All The Best —

James F. Hodgson

Engineering
Corporate Success

Engineering Corporate Success

James Hardymon

Edited by Terry L. Birdwhistell

south limestone

Published by South Limestone Books
An imprint of the University Press of Kentucky

Copyright © 2019 by The University Press of Kentucky

Editorial and Sales Offices: The University Press of Kentucky
663 South Limestone Street, Lexington, Kentucky 40508-4008
www.kentuckypress.com

Cataloging-in-Publication data available from the Library of Congress

ISBN 978-1-94-966906-0 (hardcover : alk. paper)
ISBN 978-1-94-966906-0 (pdf)
ISBN 978-1-94-966908-4 (epub)

This book is printed on acid-free paper meeting
the requirements of the American National Standard
for Permanence in Paper for Printed Library Materials.

Manufactured in the United States of America.

For my family

Contents

Photographs follow page 82

Foreword

It was 2011. The University of Kentucky faced an inflection point. Our challenges, and the decisions we would make in confronting them, would determine our path forward for generations to come. In consultation with our board of trustees, we realized that in order to strengthen our university's competitive advantage recruiting students to our campus, we had to identify a path to rebuild key parts of our infrastructure. The board directed that we explore creative solutions, including partnerships with the private sector, to overcome numerous regulatory and fiscal challenges. So we began to investigate potential opportunities with publicly traded companies.

And so we turned, as we had in the past, to James F. Hardymon. Jim brought to the task the unique and essential perspective born of his experience as chief executive officer of Textron and his service on our board of trustees, including time as chair.

With Jim's guidance, expertise, and entrepreneurial spirit, UK boldly went to the market for a solution. We needed to act quickly, with an equally committed and visionary partner, to secure our future. Without Jim's support, what followed may not have been possible—more than $2.3 billion invested in our campus since 2011, including a bold, unprecedented partnership with private housing developer EdR.

In partnership with EdR, in only four years we constructed more than sixty-five hundred modern residence hall beds and more than two hundred active learning spaces for our students.

In the past, public universities had dabbled in public-private partnerships to build or construct one or two new facilities. But no public university had gone to the market to construct all new student housing. Nothing of that scale and scope had ever been attempted.

But Jim knew that bold action was required. What gave him such foresight? Jim understands, from years leading some of the country's largest and most successful corporations, that change and disruption are inevitable perhaps even necessary. He also understands that you either lead change in a way that benefits your company or institution, or your competition will lead. In other words, when opportunity knocks, you must be prepared to answer.

Jim's strategic leadership in this transformative partnership was motivated by his own educational experience at UK, which afforded him a pathway to success. He has a passion for ensuring that others have the same opportunities. He realized that his college education became a pathway that, combined with hard work and commitment, would lead to professional opportunities. Acting with the grit he learned from his grandfather and father, and the strength of character and compassion instilled in him by his mother, Jim helped transform his university into a gateway of hope for generations to come.

My first and fondest interactions with Jim were during the request for proposals process that ultimately led to our student housing partnership. Jim was particularly suited for the task at hand, and in the course of our time together, we found clear examples where UK's strategic priorities and Jim's passions aligned. Most evident from our experience is Jim's deep personal interest in and commitment to the success of our students and his alma mater, Kentucky's flagship university.

Jim's deep Kentucky roots and his philanthropic commitment to Kentucky and to UK extend over decades. Jim and Gay Hardymon's generosity has provided for a technology-rich academic experience, supported advanced clinical care, and invested in support programs that enhance the success of our students.

Over the last several years, Jim has generously shared with me the fundamental building blocks to his success, something I have eagerly encouraged him to share with our students. He encourages everyone to "investigate carefully a prospective academic and career path, develop robust public speaking and presentation skills, maintain your health, and take the time to build a diverse skill set." And based on his life experiences, I know Jim would add, "Never overlook the importance of family, both those who helped mold you and the important role you play in your children's and grandchildren's lives."

Jim is proud of his commitment to the university and the purposeful choices he has made to help ensure our success. Twice a member of our board of trustees and serving one term as chair, he brought new insights and corporate procedures to the board during a significant, and often politically fraught era in UK's history and development. His commitment to the university, and to education more broadly, is rooted in having witnessed the positive impact of a community college in his hometown of Maysville, Kentucky, his personal experience as a UK student, and his belief in UK's vital leadership role.

Jim made these commitments because he believes the Commonwealth requires and benefits from UK's unique capacity to help grow the state's economy; create an educated, high-tech, and highly skilled workforce; and address the significant health challenges that have plagued Kentucky for far too long. An educated Kentucky is simply a better Kentucky.

Early in this memoir, Jim recalls, "The Hardymons always seemed to be building something." In his life, Jim has helped build a strong family, multiple successful companies, and the University of Kentucky. On our campus, he is responsible not simply for the buildings that bear his name but for the generations of students who traverse our campus building their futures. Because of him, the UK family is better prepared for when opportunity knocks. Because of Jim, we are prepared to answer.

Eli Capilouto
President, University of Kentucky

Editor's Preface

This memoir began as a series of oral history interviews I conducted with James F. Hardymon. The nearly twenty-five hours of interviews were recorded between February 2009 and February 2018. They are archived in the Louie B. Nunn Center for Oral History at the University of Kentucky Libraries. Over the course of two years, Mr. Hardymon and I transformed the interview transcripts into this memoir. Showing the same dedication that allowed him to succeed in business, Mr. Hardymon worked hard to assure that this memoir accurately represents his life story.

The Nunn Center for Oral History is recognized internationally as a leader and innovator in the collection and preservation of oral histories. The thousands of history interviews in the collection provide a unique look into Kentucky and American history and culture and represent an irreplaceable resource for researchers today and for generations to come. The collections focus on twentieth- and twenty-first-century Kentucky history, Appalachia, Kentucky writers, agriculture, African American history, the history of education, politics and public policy, military veterans, healthcare, business, and the history of the University of Kentucky.

Terry L. Birdwhistell
Senior Oral Historian and
former Dean of UK Libraries

Acknowledgments

This memoir benefited from the support of the faculty and staff of the University of Kentucky Libraries and the Louie B. Nunn Center for Oral History including Doug Boyd, Kopana Terry, Danielle Gabbard, Sarah Dorpinghaus, Crystal Heis, Shell Dunn, and Jason Flahardy. University of Kentucky staff Jay Blanton, Mark Cornelison, Kelly Hahn, and Aaron Camenisch provided help in securing images. Thanks to Janice Birdwhistell for reviewing the manuscript in its various stages. Thanks also to Kathy Gaynor of Webster University for providing the photograph of Larry Browning.

Finally, thanks to the University Press of Kentucky staff Leila Salisbury, Patricia Weber, Robin DuBlanc, and Tasha Huber for providing their professional publishing expertise to this memoir.

Chapter One

Beginning at the River

My earliest childhood memories are of floods.

My life journey began on the banks of the Ohio River in Maysville, Kentucky, founded in the late eighteenth century by pioneers Simon Kenton and Daniel Boone, among others. Roughly sixty miles northeast of Lexington, this small river town became an important entryway for early settlers making their way into the Bluegrass State. Decades later Maysville became a stop on the Underground Railroad as slaves sought freedom across the river. Over time, Maysville became a thriving tobacco and hemp market.

My parents, Kenneth T. and Pauline Strode Hardymon, married in 1930. I arrived in the midst of the Great Depression on Armistice Day in 1934. They named me for my grandfather, James Franklin Hardymon. Everyone called him Frank, but I was known as Jimmy. We lived in a little house on Cottage Street on the eastern side of Maysville. The land in that section of town slopes down to the river and Cottage Street ended at the river. There were four adjacent houses on the street that had all been constructed by Hardymons. We lived in the last house on the street, closest to the river.

My earliest childhood memories are of floods. Every two or three years the fast-rising flood waters of the Ohio River forced us out of our house. Each time all of our possessions had to be moved from the basement to the second floor of the house. But during the historic 1937 flood, water even reached the top floor. I can vividly recall looking down our basement steps and seeing the water rising one step at a time up into the house. Thankfully, we moved to higher ground two years later. While we were not as directly impacted by later floods, the 1945 flood inundated half of Maysville, and I vividly remember residents cruising the downtown streets of Maysville in motorboats.

Family lore has it that my grandfather Frank and my grandmother Francis "Fanny" Barbour Hardymon arrived in Maysville from neighboring Lewis County in the early 1900s with seven children and only $100. Back then the two most important things for success were land and tobacco. Over time the family became heavily involved in growing tobacco. They acquired tobacco-auctioning warehouses and operated two businesses in Maysville, including a tobacco re-dryer operation.

The Hardymon lumber business grew out of the need for timber during World War II. The Hardymons cut timber on some of the land they owned in Kentucky and Ohio and began selling it. Granddad soon expanded the lumberyard by also selling sand and gravel. He had loaned money to a group of men that supplied him with sand and gravel. At some point the men owed Granddad so much money that he soon owned about 65 percent of their business and eventually bought the entire concern. The sand and gravel business still exists today, although the only family member still involved is one of my cousins.

Granddad pursued many business ventures, including operating the Maysville bus line during World War II. Business flourished because wartime gas rationing limited driving personal cars and trucks. Of course, the war also made it very difficult to maintain the buses because of the shortages of parts. A benefit of Granddad owning the bus company was that I got to ride the bus for free. But the downside was that my teacher, Flossie Jones, often teased me during school because the bus would often break down, making her late for work. Her teasing did not bother me that much except that it brought the kind of attention to me that, as a kid, I really did not need. The Hardymons got out of the bus business after the war ended.

As Granddad developed and owned businesses, he became recognized in Maysville and the surrounding area as a community leader. He was very involved in the planning and construction of Maysville's floodwall and went to Washington, D.C., with other community leaders numerous times to seek funding for the floodwall project. Granddad always seemed to be doing interesting things. Even after he "retired" to Florida he was not one to simply sit around and relax. While in Florida he bought and maintained rental houses and was always thinking and planning for the next big thing.

Dad was the third oldest of seven children. It seemed every family member had some kind of role in the family enterprises because Granddad liked to keep his family close. The Hardymon businesses were family owned and operated and utilized a very archaic method of joint ownership. My aunt Lillian Rains, another person who had a great influence on me, was a whiz with numbers and maintained all of the account books for the Harydmon businesses. She amazed me with her ability to talk on the telephone while adding a column of numbers in a time before anybody in Maysville ever thought about calculators.

Whatever cash each individual family had was tied up in the businesses. So you had to go to Aunt Lillian if you wanted money to purchase anything. For example, if one family wanted to buy a refrigerator, or anything that was more than the cost of weekly groceries, they had to ask for the money from the business. Not surprisingly, that financial arrangement created some interesting discussions around our dinner table. The family's approach to "revenue sharing" made a huge impression on me and may have been a key reason I chose not to join the family businesses years later. Nevertheless, the system seemed to work well for the Hardymons for many years.

One of Dad's six siblings, Walter, died of pneumonia in 1932 while attending the University of Kentucky. Two of his other siblings did not go into the family business, but they still had some cash in the business. Uncle Phillip, who was five years younger than Dad, became a physician and practiced in Columbus while also serving as team physician for the Ohio State University football team. We used to go up to one Ohio State football game every year. Uncle Phillip always encouraged me to go to college.

Some of my cousins recall fishing trips with Granddad, but I have no such memories. My grandfather did not have a lot of idle time so instead of fishing together, we might go out to check on the cattle on one of the farms. I have very wonderful memories of spending time with Granddad as he checked on his many businesses.

Granddad seemed to enjoy his role as family patriarch. Every Sunday afternoon during the summer the extended family gathered behind Granddad's house where he had a little building and a tennis court. The family also celebrated every Thanksgiving, Christmas, and New Year's at Granddad's house. His role was like a commander in chief for the Hardymon family.

I was only fifteen when Granddad died, but he left an imprint on me that I only came to truly appreciate as I grew older and began to reflect on the major influences in my life. He was more of an entrepreneur than I am, but I believe he passed on to me the desire to lead and to build businesses.

When I became involved in international corporations I sometimes reflected back on Granddad developing his businesses in Maysville. I suppose we both had an inclination toward business and that is why my Granddad and I became very close. I was the oldest grandchild and he probably did not have as much time to spend with all of the grandchildren as he had with me.

In contrast to Granddad's entrepreneurial spirit, my father had a steadier and more methodical approach to his work. Dad finished high school but began working nearly full-time on the various Hardymon construction projects when he turned fourteen. I do not recall Dad ever expressing any regret about not going to college. I remember how proud he was that he had attended a week-long class at the Ohio Mechanical Institute, where he learned to read blueprints. Even though two younger brothers had attended college, Dad must have felt some need or desire to begin working in the family businesses right out of high school. In Maysville at that time it was seen as a normal progression for a young man.

Dad was honest and worked hard his entire life. The term *hard worker* meant something to him and he was proud of the label. I admired Dad and considered him a great man. He came of age at a time when it was important to Granddad that someone dig in pretty quickly to help with the family's businesses. I think Granddad chose Aunt Lillian and Dad because they were the oldest, even though both certainly had the intelligence to do well in college. It was just expected and accepted that the family businesses came first.

Even though Dad was a really good father, one could never satisfy him. He did not like to set specific goals because he always believed more could be accomplished. A few years after Gay and I married I remember her asking Dad, "Papaw, why are you always so negative and picking on Jim?" His reply summed up Dad pretty well: "You don't brag on a good horse." That might have been the highest compliment I ever received from my father. I am sure Dad was proud that I earned an engineering degree but I never thought he had a clue what I did at work all day until I became president of a company. He assumed that I mostly shuffled papers around an office desk. He truly did not understand the workings of larger companies and corporations.

I remember Mother always being there for me throughout my childhood. As an only child, I received plenty of her attention. She handled the discipline in our family and kept tight reins on me. Mother was an absolutely wonderful person with a great sense of humor. She lived to be ninety-one years old and remained alert and active until the end.

Following Granddad's death in 1950, the family businesses

continued to run the same as if he was still in charge. Dad operated the farms, Aunt Lillian managed the finances, and Uncle Glen ran the lumber business. Without Granddad there was probably a little less oversight of the total operation but that was the only change. There continued to be two distinct workforces for the farms and the businesses, but only one payroll system.

The businesses became a little more cautious in terms of expanding, drawing their horns in a little. For instance, one of the ventures that did not work out very well was acquisition of a tobacco re-drying operation. Re-drying is a process that takes the juice out of the tobacco, which is then stored for about three years before it goes to the cigarette manufacturers. Tobacco re-drying turned out to be one of Granddad's least successful ventures so the family drew back to the core farming and businesses.

A major part of the farm operation was raising cattle. But Dad also got into owning and breeding Tennessee Walking Horses, which had become very popular. Many people, instead of owning boats or motorcycles, had a riding horse, and a Tennessee Walking Horse was generally a smooth riding horse. Dad's interest in horses evolved into a small business. In those days one could keep a stable in town and we had fourteen horse stalls adjacent to the lumberyard. We also kept stallions and brood mares out on the farm and we would breed them and then break the young horses. I enjoyed many summer evenings riding our horses in an area that ran parallel to the Ohio River.

We attended numerous horse shows in Kentucky and beyond to promote our horses. Every September as part of our family vacation, we traveled to Shelbyville, Tennessee, which was the site of the World's Championship Walking Horse competition. We also advertised our Tennessee Walkers in several magazines. One day a car pulled up with a Pennsylvania license plate and fins on the back of the car so tall they looked like an airplane tail. A tall, rangy fellow wearing a hat and a girl about my age who turned out to be his daughter got out of the car. As a chubby twelve-year-old boy I stood watching this event unfold with great curiosity.

The man and his daughter spent some time examining a particular horse and eventually asked Dad if the horse had been broken and if he was gentle to ride. About that time I walked around the corner of the barn and Dad said, "Yeah, even this kid can ride him." Before I knew what was happening, Dad had a saddle on that horse and he put me up on it with the stirrups about a foot too long for my legs. I had never been on that particular horse but I rode it around for the man and his daughter and tried my best to look good doing it. I must have succeeded because they bought the horse.

Horses then might sell for $700 or $800, which would be a little over $9,000 today. Unfortunately, the Tennessee Walking Horse business gradually declined. As in all businesses, one has to have a business plan, and I am certain that Dad did not have a plan for our horse business. Peoples' interests changed and it became increasingly difficult to sell our horses. We eventually just turned the last three or four horses loose on the farm. But our horse business venture made a deep and lasting impression on me. In business, one cannot just do the same thing over and over and over and expect to succeed in the long term. Back then I had no way of knowing that I had just learned a valuable lesson about exit strategy. I also realized later that one can learn valuable life lessons anywhere simply by paying attention to what is happening around you.

I was only seven years old when the Japanese bombed Pearl Harbor. I vividly remember learning that someone from our community had died in the war. In such a small town, every casualty made a huge impact. The stories and images of the war we saw on the movie newsreels on Saturdays brought the war even closer. However, my most lasting memories of the war are the letters Uncle Jim Hardymon wrote me from the battlefield. He served under General Patton as an enlisted man walking behind a tank. His letters arrived with parts of them blacked out for security reasons.

I will never forget the day I learned Uncle Jim had been killed. I was sitting with friends in church one Sunday morning in July 1944 when I noticed a person I did not know come into the church and escort my grandmother out during the service. I knew that was highly unusual and I could not imagine what it meant. My parents were not in church that Sunday but when I got home they told me that Uncle Jim had been killed. The news upset me terribly, and even to this day, I find it hard to talk about Uncle Jim without becoming very emotional.

Dad was thirty-three when the war began and as it continued, many older men were drafted. But since Dad kept getting older, too, he was never drafted. I really do not recall much discussion, if any, within the family about the prospect of him going into the military. I never asked him if not going into the service ever bothered him. There never seemed to be any conflict within the family about who went to war and who stayed home.

When we learned of the Japanese surrender, people drove their cars up and down the streets blowing their horns. Everyone was shouting and celebrating the wonderful news. Then, seemingly overnight, life just slid back into a normal routine. Uncle Jim's widow was not around very much, and as far as I knew she went on with her life. Uncle Glen came home from the navy and resumed his role in the family lumber business.

Military service remained a large part of the lives of many boys from Maysville as the country moved from World War II into the Korean War. When I graduated from high school, for example, probably 30 percent of my male classmates entered the military. The Korean War did not have the same impact on Maysville as World War II, but it was still a war and our boys were at risk.

I have always thought that more people should have the opportunity to experience the discipline the military offers even though I did not personally like it. In the military we always knew what we were going to do. We knew we had to carry out an order even if it we thought it was stupid. The military did not allow one to ask, "What do you mean?"

Probably in part because I was an only child, I could hardly wait to start school. In those days Maysville had four elementary schools located around the town. I walked a block to school for grades 1 through 3. First and second grades met in the same room, with first-graders sitting on one side of the room and second-graders on the other. I always thought that arrangement really helped me academically because I was able to hear the second-grade lesson while I was supposed to be listening to the first-grade teacher. For some odd reason my first school only had grades 1, 2, 3, and 6 so for fourth and fifth grades I moved to a school a little further away, to which I rode my bike. For sixth grade I returned to the school nearest to my home.

Grades 7-12 were downtown at Maysville High School, which had about 320 students. My graduating class had 45 students. I did well in school and I usually served as a class officer, joined several student clubs, and participated in school plays. But Mother and Dad evidently hoped to expand my horizons even more so they signed me up for piano lessons. Unfortunately, that cultural experiment did not last very long. Later, a man came to Maysville promoting a type of wind instrument that he claimed would provide a good background for playing other wind instruments. Mother and Dad paid a minimum amount for me to practice the instrument under the man's guidance, as did several other families. About a month into the lessons the man gathered up the instruments from us, saying that he needed to clean them. Well, he left town and we never heard from him again. That early lesson in theft and fraud made quite an impression on me.

I liked basketball and baseball so I tried out for the high school teams. Maysville High did not field a football team, and at that time there were no sports for girls. I had some success with baseball, playing on the school team and during the summer in independent leagues. Baseball probably interested me more because I could play it fairly well and I was too short and too slow for basketball. I played third base on our high school baseball team and on the independent teams I played either second or third base. We played teams from nearby communities like Tollesboro, Flemingsburg, and Vanceburg. On occasion we would venture out to play teams near Cincinnati and we would get trimmed pretty well.

Even though I really liked baseball and the Cincinnati Reds were relatively close by, I did not attend many of their games. Major league baseball did not really interest Mother and Dad. But Uncle Glen was a very big sports fan and we always talked sports and that kept me interested. I also listened to Reds games on the radio. I do not remember exactly when I saw my first Cincinnati Reds baseball game but I do recall watching Ted Williams throw out the first pitch at the 1953 all-star game in Cincinnati, even though he was not on an active roster due to military service.

I served as manager of the high school basketball team in 1948 and 1949. Earle Jones coached the Maysville basketball team and to this day holds the record for most state tournament wins. Maysville won the state championship in 1947, beating Brewers High School from Marshall County in the championship game of the state tournament by a score of 54–40. Maysville had high hopes for another championship in 1948 but we faced a rematch with Brewers High School in the championship game. This time the Brewers won, ending their season undefeated.

The Maysville radio station's call letters, WFTM, stood for "World's Finest Tobacco Market." The Finch family owned and operated the station, which was located in an old tobacco warehouse. Coach Jones hosted a sports program on the station weekdays at 6:15 p.m. The basketball team practiced until around 6, and then Coach Jones and I would hustle over to the radio station, which was about four blocks from our house.

After arriving at the station only minutes before we went on the air live, Coach would have me scurrying around pulling together material for that day's show. He discussed the Maysville High School basketball team and local sports in general. During the show I would be right outside the studio, still gathering additional material he could use. During a commercial break I would rush in and hand it to him, but I never got on the air. Coach Jones became a mentor to me and was someone I truly looked up to.

I enjoyed school but each fall I dreaded transitioning from summer work back to school. My summer jobs were mostly manual labor and driving dump trucks, but I liked working in the family businesses and associating with the other workers. Those summers instilled in me the value of hard work and significantly influenced my life and the way I would approach business.

I also enjoyed working with Dad on the farm. But he would never let me cut or hang tobacco because it was dangerous work. My work in tobacco consisted mostly of picking the tobacco up out of the field once it had been cut and taking it to the barn, where I would stand on the truck and lift the tobacco up to be hung. I was a small, short kid and I suppose Dad did not want me to fall out of the barn. But being on the bottom rung of the process meant that pieces of tobacco fell back down on me the entire day. I also vividly recall bringing bailed hay in from hot fields in the middle of summer. It did not take much of that kind of work to convince me that perhaps school was not that bad.

Since I had not learned to swim, I did not especially like time spent on the river working on my family's two boats that were used for towing sand and gravel barges. I also drove a dump truck, hauling construction materials for use in building the Maysville floodwall. We supplied sand and gravel for the concrete portion of the wall. I remember doing things I would not dare do now. For example, they were building up low places in some areas simply with dirt and constructing a levy, not using concrete. They used what they called brick-back, which was basically rocks, to fill in between the rows of dirt. So my truck, with me in it, would be lowered down near the water where I would dump the load. Then, using a cable, they would pull me and the truck back up the hill. It was dangerous work but I just did not think much about it at the time.

I have very fond memories of those summers, and the people I worked with made a lasting impression on me. I observed working families living from paycheck to paycheck. I doubt that I would have ever truly appreciated the many challenges blue-collar workers face had I not seen it firsthand. Most of the hourly workers did not even have checking accounts. Each Friday after being paid, they took their checks and cashed them somewhere in town. By the end of the following work week they would sometimes have to borrow money against their next check. That said, many of the workers seemed to enjoy life and not dwell on anything negative. *Salt of the earth* is the term that comes to mind when I think back about my co-workers from those summers. They worked hard, smoked, and looked old before their time.

Any small town has a class hierarchy and Maysville was no exception. I saw it from two angles. The nicest residential area in Maysville was Edgemont, situated on the hill above Maysville on the road to Lexington. It was obvious that the residents of Edgemont were the businesspeople of the community, the owners of what became Browning Manufacturing and of January Wood, which made yarn and thread, as well as the leading tobacco people in the community.

Edgemont children usually went away to boarding schools, but I became acquainted with some of them before they left. I generally played down any connections I might have with the wealthier kids because I preferred being just "one of the gang." I strove to get along with everyone and usually did. Many of the kids I regularly played pick-up ball games with were children of working-class laborers who may have been struggling financially and not sure where they might get their next meal.

And, unfortunately, we attended segregated schools that perpetuated another deep chasm in the formal social structure of the community. African Americans attended the John G. Fee High School, which was named for the Reverend John G. Fee (1816–1901), founder of Berea College, who was an abolitionist and started the first racially integrated school in Kentucky. Most of my friendships with African Americans came through sports, especially baseball. Of course, Jackie Robinson made a huge impression on me because he was such a great player and integrated the major leagues. I was fortunate to see him play in Cincinnati a couple of times during his career.

When my friends and I were not in school, playing sports, or working, we could often be found just hanging out in downtown Maysville, which boasted a wide variety of stores that would stay open late on Friday evenings. In addition to watching movies at the Russell Theater, we would gather at Vance's drugstore and drink sodas. We would slide into a booth and stay until we were run out for making too much noise or not spending enough money. On nice days we would stand around on the corner outside the drugstore. We had to amuse ourselves because there just was not that much to do in Maysville. Even television came relatively late to our town. But eventually people began erecting antennas that could pull in the Cincinnati stations. The people who lived up on the hill surrounding Maysville had two distinct advantages: their homes did not flood and it was easier to get television reception. But we listened to a lot of radio. I can remember sitting in our living room with Mother and Dad listening to Jack Benny and programs like *Fibber McGee and Molly.*

Of course, like boys everywhere, we still found time for some mischief, and I can easily remember when I got into the most trouble. During the fall and early winter after the tobacco had been brought to market, Mother worked at the tobacco warehouse weighing tobacco. That meant that between 3:30 and 6:00 in the afternoons I was often home alone. One winter day three of us were returning from shooting at cans with our BB guns down along the river. Suddenly, the police pulled up, took our guns, and loaded the three of us into the back of the cruiser behind the cage partition.

At the police station they accused us of shooting out streetlights and put us in a small jail cell with no place to sit. They also took our BBs and threw them in the trash can. That was most upsetting because BBs were really hard to come by back then. The police officers reprimanded us pretty sternly, and Tommy Whitaker admitted that he had shot out the streetlights. Even though I had not shot out any streetlight, I was guilty by association.

Eventually they took us out of the cell, piled us all back into the police car, and drove us home. By the time I got home it was long past the time I should have been there. I walked in the house and decided the best thing to do was to lay the entire story out for Mother and Dad. The next day all three of us boys had to go to the Kentucky Utilities office in Maysville and apologize for shooting out their streetlights. I dutifully apologized even though I had not done a thing. And, as one might suspect, that was the end of my BB gun days. Mother and Dad were really not into corporal punishment. They knew that shame was always most effective with me.

Every boy in Maysville—and many men, for that matter—seemed to have a nickname. For example, among my classmates were "Beak" Barkley, "Ears" Barnett, and "Sniffles" Weaver. Once, while playing basketball in junior high, a chubby fellow and I got tangled up, resulting in a jump ball. As the two of us lined up for the jump, Coach Jones looked at the two of us and remarked, "Well, here's 'Fats' and 'Foots.'" Coach called me "Foots" because my feet were so small that I had to wear special shoes as a kid. From that day on the nickname Foots followed me all through high school and even beyond.

Years later Nick Clooney, a Maysville native and father of George Clooney, once wrote a column for the Cincinnati paper about nicknames. To my surprise he shared with his readers, "I once knew a guy who went by the nickname of 'Foots.' He is now CEO of one of the largest corporations in America." Fortunately, he did not share my real name in the article. But when I returned to Maysville to be honored as a distinguished alumnus of Maysville High School, Coach Jones, who had become the principal, still introduced me as Foots Hardymon.

My senior class in high school had roughly forty-five students, divided equally between girls and boys. Some of us had been together in class since the first grade, so it was a fairly close-knit group. By the time I reached high school, I realized that I was good in math and I enjoyed those classes and did well. I also made good grades in science classes. While I did not make straight As in high school, I did well enough to be named valedictorian of my class, which was a tremendous honor. Fortunately, I did not have to give a speech at the graduation ceremony. But, I am sure to my parents' delight, I did go up on the stage that hot June night to be recognized.

In addition to being involved in high school sports, I also had parts in the junior and senior class plays. That is not to say I thought I had a future in acting, but with so few students, everyone had to participate in most of the school events. I had roles in plays from the third grade through high school, even though I never really enjoyed doing it. But I never landed a leading role in a play. I remember in *Cinderella* I played the role of the person who put the shoe on Cinderella. On another occasion in high school, mine and another boy's parts required us to dress like girls. I still remember the Walter Scott line from the play, "Oh, what a tangled web we weave, when first we practice to deceive." I did not deliver that line in the play but I never forgot it.

When I reflect back on my youth, I realize how fortunate I was to have the family I did and to live in a place like Maysville. Back then, Maysville had a population of roughly sixty-five hundred people. The town was fifty miles in any direction from a larger city. Many people never ventured very far from Maysville. It was a very safe community and we walked or rode our bicycles everywhere. There were no drugs that I knew about. A kid like me went to school, went to church, worked, and played sports. Those activities made up the rhythm of our lives.

My wonderful parents provided for me, encouraged me, and sent me to school. That is a great advantage for a young person. While Mother and Dad were not rich, even by Maysville standards, we were comfortable and they made sure I had what I needed. And even in death, Granddad continued his influence on my life.

In his will, he left $9,000 to each of his eleven grandchildren. We received the money when we turned twenty-one and I have never forgotten how much his generosity helped me to succeed in life.

Even though I always thought I would go to college, I spent very little time planning for it. During my senior year in high school I received brochures from several colleges, which I am certain my classmates also received. Since neither of my parents had attended college, they really wanted me to earn a college degree. Uncle Phil, the physician, also encouraged me to go to college. I had learned from Dad the satisfaction and rewards of hard work. If I had chosen to delay college, work in the family businesses, develop an even stronger work ethic, I think Dad would have supported me.

Nevertheless, even though I never found school very appealing, by August following high school graduation I had decided to attend the University of Kentucky. I probably chose UK because it was the easiest decision to make. All I had to do was tell them I was coming and then show up. If there were any summer orientations or campus tours I did not know about them. I received a letter telling me my "application for admittance had been approved."

The Sunday after Labor Day, 1952, Mother and Dad drove me to Lexington. I was only seventeen years old and terribly green. I was so late in deciding to enroll at UK that there were no dormitory rooms left. So I rented a room from a woman who lived on Aylesford Place, a street near campus between Rose Lane and Maxwell Street.

I boarded with two other students on the second floor. I had to adapt because as an only child I was unaccustomed to sharing living spaces. We had separate bedrooms but shared a bath down the hall. One of my housemates was Barkley Sturgill, an older student who was studying for the bar exam. The other was Ted Phillips, who was from Louisville and a couple of years older than me.

Unlike today's college student, I had very little to unpack when I got into my room. I doubt that I even brought a radio with me. On my own for the first time in my life that first night at college, I walked the one mile to the downtown Ben Ali Theater to watch a movie. I am stretching my memory, but I am fairly certain it was a John Wayne movie.

Registering for classes the following day in Memorial Coliseum was a very trying ordeal. Rows of tables representing various majors and programs filled the basketball floor. Long lines of students trying to register formed in front of each table. Often, I would finally reach the person sitting at a desired table only to be told that the class I wanted was full. I found the entire registration process terribly frustrating.

My first college class, an English course, met in the new Fine Arts Building opened only two years earlier. The professor instructed us to write an essay about our summer experiences and undoubtedly, I wrote about my summer jobs. My toughest teacher that first year was Professor J. R. Mitchell, who taught chemistry at UK from 1917 to 1955. Long before the current emphasis on all students succeeding, Professor Mitchell took a different approach. Each semester on the first day of his classes, he would say, "Look to your right, look to your left. One of you won't be here by Thanksgiving." Professor Mitchell and chemistry were very tough on me, but I survived.

I think I chose engineering as a major because it seemed to relate most closely to our family businesses. The Hardymons always seemed to be building something. Moreover, UK offered a limited number of degree programs compared to today, and civil engineering was recognized as one of UK's top academic areas. Because of Sputnik and the ensuing "space race," the federal government sought more engineering graduates and I received a lot of encouragement from the faculty.

My academic career began slowly and modestly. While I was never in any academic trouble, it quickly became apparent to me that my high school science background was woefully insufficient. Maysville High was stronger in other areas and actually improved its science education over time. But once I decided to major in engineering I stuck with it. UK required eighteen to twenty hours of electives so I took courses like geology and political science. I tried never to venture very far away from engineering and mathematics. For example, I did not elect to take art or similar courses.

I had not given much thought to the social aspects of college life and I had never been much of a joiner of social groups. But once I settled into college life, I decided to pledge the Sigma Alpha Epsilon fraternity, which was somewhat out of character for me. Uncle Jim had been a Kappa Sigma at UK. Several men I knew back in Maysville belonged to Sigma Alpha Epsilon, but no one else from Maysville pledged SAE during my time in the fraternity. I went through rush at the very beginning of my first semester and pledged SAE, whose house was on South Limestone between Maxwell and High Streets.

I did not enjoy my pledge experience. Fraternities at that time hazed much more than is allowed today, and that was certainly something I was not used to. The actives engaged more in silly harassment than in physical hazing. For example, they would make us get up and sing before a group or perform some similar demeaning activity that made me very uncomfortable. In 1952 many of the fraternity members were World War II veterans and that created a sizeable age difference between someone like me at seventeen, intimidating me even more.

In spite of the pledging experience, I believe my fraternity involvement became a lifesaver for me in that it offered a pathway for leadership and socializing on a scale I had never experienced. We were required to have dinner at the fraternity house one night each week. I also began having lunch there occasionally. I slowly worked my way into it and then the second year I moved into the SAE house. That move changed my entire outlook towards the fraternity.

Unlike some of my fellow students, I did not have to hold down any part-time jobs as an undergraduate because Mother and Dad took care of my expenses. Even though tuition was only $65 a semester and my room and board was modest, I am not really sure how much of a financial strain college put on them. I think my parents recognized that I needed time to study because I did more memorizing than learning and memorizing takes a lot of effort. I always read my assignment several times. I never really felt completely prepared, so I spent a lot of time studying, particularly during my first two years in college.

Even though I utilized the Margaret I. King Library regularly, I studied primarily in my room. I was very fortunate to have fellow boarders and later fraternity roommates who were also really good students. I roomed with the same person the entire time I lived in the fraternity house. We had a third person in the room one year, but we tried not to bother one another. We usually went to our corner of the room and studied at a little desk. Of course, college offers many distractions if you are looking for one like a card game next door.

Since UK offered no formal academic advising system back then, I turned to Professor Robert Shaver when I needed help. An accomplished and highly regarded professor and head of civil engineering, he later became dean of the College of Engineering. When I met with Professor Shaver I always felt a little intimidated, but he knew some people in Maysville and that made it easier. I think he also noticed early on that I did not cause any trouble. I looked up to Professor Shaver not as a mentor, but as someone I could always go to for advice. A couple of other engineering professors, Professor Staley Adams and Professor Jim Leggett, made positive impressions on me as well. Professor Leggett was a World War II veteran and a former prisoner of war in the Pacific who everyone respected.

I had very little trouble with most required courses, but I did have one little problem. Even though I had grown up next to the Ohio River I had never learned to swim and passing a swimming proficiency was required to graduate. I became very concerned that swimming, of all things, could keep me from graduating. Professor Shaver did not offer much reassurance when he told me, "You're worrying yourself about something that I don't know if you're going to accomplish or not." Fortunately, UK waived the swimming requirement for me. I suspect Professor Shaver had something to do with that. I successfully completed the rest of the physical education course, minus the swimming.

Intramurals became very important to me, especially after I began participating on the fraternity teams. SAE always wanted to win any type of competitive event and we won more than our share during my time in the fraternity, both athletic and otherwise. I enjoyed the competition, especially softball, and that probably accelerated my involvement in fraternity life more than formal dances or other social events.

I did not become SAE president until I was in graduate school, which was somewhat unusual. By that time I had lived in the SAE house for three years. I lost my initial bid for president but won the second time. My graduate class and work schedule was such that it was actually a better time for me to take on more fraternity responsibilities.

As fraternity president I learned a great deal about leadership. Running our fraternity meetings was never easy because it was a lot like herding cats. At any particular meeting I could expect a squabble over something among the members. But it was good training, in part because the discipline aspect of the job was very new to me. As president I was ultimately responsible for enforcing proper behavior in the house, including prohibiting drinking. I made it a point not to go snooping around and I made sure to knock loudly before entering anyone's room.

Other, much more serious experiences became part of my maturing process. Danny Woodward, a fraternity brother who had earlier served as president, died tragically. While ice-skating at the city reservoir he fell through the ice and drowned. Harry McChesney, a law school friend, attempted to rescue Danny but he, too, fell through the ice and drowned. The fraternity members attended the funeral and, as one might expect, the grief among the brothers became overwhelming. Those types of life experiences leave their mark on a leader.

Some of my most beneficial fraternity experiences were actually business related. For example, we knew that our house on South Limestone was in such bad shape that it would one day likely either burn down or simply fall down. While I was president we arranged to sell our property to the L. R. Cooke Chevrolet dealership adjacent to our property. Then we struck a deal with UK for a long-term lease for a house on campus. That house has been replaced as well.

Another important presidential responsibility was dealing with our housemother, Mrs. Bennie G. Williams. Of course, we thought we did not need a housemother but Mom Williams was a very good one and very nice to us. Our biggest squabbles were always over meals. It is impossible to satisfy forty-five young men eating two or three meals a day at the same place. But I worked well with Mom Williams and occasionally visited with her in her apartment to see how she was doing and exchange ideas.

I also participated in a ten-day SAE leadership workshop in Evanston, Illinois, the summer between my junior and senior years. That was a big trip for me. The workshop leaders spent a lot of time telling us how valuable the SAE experience was going to be in our personal lives and where it would lead us in our professional lives. That said, I do not remember a single time in my business career when after the secret handshake a fraternity brother said, "I am going to work with you because we are fraternity brothers." Still, my fraternity experience meant more to me than any other part of college life.

Many people look back on their college years as the best time of their life. But for me, college was just not that exciting. Perhaps that is because my time in business was so much more exciting and enjoyable. I actually approached college as one would one's first job. I made no real connection to the university as a student, and the college experiences I had could have happened on any campus. I simply went about college in a workmanlike fashion. As I reflect back on my college experience, perhaps I did not get as much out of it as I could have.

I graduated from UK with a bachelor's degree in civil engineering in August 1956. Following graduation I had to make a decision about whether to go back to the family business in Maysville or start interviewing for other positions. The most attractive jobs at that time were with the oil companies, which seemed to be taking anyone with an engineering degree. People I respected were urging me to go to graduate school and offering me a way to help pay for it.

Dean Shaver and members of the engineering faculty introduced me to the leaders of the Kentucky Highway Research group, which was located near the UK campus. They told me about a program initiated by Kentucky governor A. B. "Happy" Chandler that selected prospective engineering students who might pursue a career in highway engineering in Kentucky. Following my interview for one of the positions, I was selected and entered graduate school in September. There were eight of us in the program and Governor Chandler invited us to Frankfort and spent some time with us.

I began work in the state highway lab in October 1956 and entered graduate school for a number of reasons. First and foremost was the military draft. I did not complete the last two years of ROTC and I suppose that I, like a lot of young men, thought the Korean War would be the last war, at least for several years. But the draft continued. I had a draft deferment as an undergraduate and I could also obtain a deferment while in graduate school. But probably the single biggest reason I chose graduate school was because I simply did not yet know what to do with my life.

I loosened up more in graduate school because I was working with the same people who had taught me as an undergraduate. I simply felt more comfortable, especially while working in the highway research lab. Also, Mother and Dad continued to support me in graduate school. I cannot emphasize enough how important their ongoing support was to my education. It gave me a real advantage.

As important, Mother and Dad never pressured me to return to Maysville and join the family businesses, perhaps because there were already so many members of the family working in the businesses. And even after earning my engineering degrees, I never tried to tell them how to run the businesses. During the summers I had always worked for Uncle Glen's side of the business more than Dad's side. Uncle Glen knew enough to realize that the business could benefit from some long-term planning. He continually encouraged me to share with him ideas for how the family businesses might expand in additional areas that would align with our work experience, skills, and finances.

A very small group within the extended family ran the businesses. I just cannot imagine what I would have done had I returned to Maysville. It would have been a shame for me to have gone back home only to end up operating a dump truck. But I knew they would try to create something for me within the family businesses that matched my education and training. I just did not feel comfortable choosing that path.

Even though the state financed my graduate work, I had no contract that required me to work for the Kentucky Highway Department for two years after finishing my graduate degree. Nevertheless, I understood it to be an unwritten commitment. Most of us knew very little about contracts but we simply understood that our commitment *was* a contract. As I advanced through the graduate engineering program and spent time in the highway laboratory, I realized that working in a state highway department or with a road contractor might be the best use of my engineering knowledge. I realized that technology was not going to be my strong suit. I also knew by then that I was not going to invent something or take part in a project that created the next big idea.

Like so many areas of engineering back then, my graduate thesis incorporated coal. My research investigated how fly ash, a coal-burning byproduct, might be useful for something. It was very difficult to figure out a way to use it productively and some fly ash ponds had actually broken loose and caused huge environmental problems. Someone proposed mixing fly ash with lime and using it for soil stabilization. The idea was to use the fly ash/lime mixture as a load-bearing road bed after the soil has been dug out. My work never went beyond lab experiments, but I would mix cubes of fly ash and then test how they held up under heavy weight such as is experienced in a road bed. My research did not change the way roads were built or improve soil stabilization. However, it was a worthwhile project because as a result of my work and that of others, the mixture began to be used for airport landing strips. My thesis was documented as a Kentucky Transportation Center Research Report: James F. Hardymon, "A Study of Lime and Fly Ash with Regard to Soil Stabilization" (1958).

After completing my graduate work in June 1958, I immediately became eligible for the draft. Realizing I would likely be drafted, I joined an Army Reserve Transportation Unit in Lexington. I also began my two-year commitment to the Kentucky Highway Department. As expected, I received my draft notice in October. Elvis followed me into the military a year later.

The Army Reserve required six months' active duty and then seven and a half years as a reserve. I began basic training at Fort Knox with 220 other men. Even counting the officers for our unit, only three of us had college degrees. Since I was twenty-three years old with a graduate degree, inevitably I became known as "Pops" or "Grandpa" by most of the seventeen- and eighteen-year-old soldiers. Basic training was not particularly difficult but it was another adjustment for me. I tried to keep up with a bunch of much younger men and live with forty or fifty people in a barracks—another major challenge for an only child. But the time passed and I made it through basic and then headed to Fort Dix, New Jersey.

I reported to Fort Dix the first week of January 1959, but upon arrival my orders were missing. They told me, "Everybody that comes here from Fort Knox basic training usually goes into advanced infantry training." Well, that sounded like a step in the wrong direction as I was wanting an improvement from basic training. So I replied, "Why don't we just wait and see if my orders show up?" Fortunately, when my orders finally arrived a few days later, I was assigned to the engineering unit. I was surprised because the army was generally known for placing soldiers in an area they knew the least about. Our primary assignment was to retrofit buildings to serve as storage facilities for nuclear ammunition.

I had driven my car to New Jersey and received permission to park it off the post. On weekends I would often go into New York City. I had been pleased to learn that a soldier in uniform always went to the front of the line in a restaurant and received tickets from the USO for theater and sporting events in Madison Square Garden. As I was being discharged Dad came up to Fort Dix on the train. We saw a couple of Broadway plays and spent some quality time together before driving back to Kentucky together in my car.

I had a good experience at Fort Dix for four months and looked forward to spending the remainder of my military commitment in the reserves. When I returned to my position with the Kentucky Highway Department, we began a variety of projects that I found most interesting. I gained a great deal of respect for the highway department during my time there. When you drive down a highway and see a state worker leaning on a shovel, you have a tendency to conclude that they do not work very hard. I suggest that everyone who thinks that should try shoveling for eight hours straight. You might conclude that leaning on that shovel occasionally is actually a necessary part of the job. There were a lot of good and dedicated people in the Kentucky Highway Department.

I also had additional exposure to Governor Chandler, which was exciting. We did a project attempting to use a coal base material called coal tar to pave roads instead of oil-based material. Governor Chandler and others believed that this would stimulate the coal industry, which was going through its usual up and down cycles. Koppers, a Pennsylvania company, sent a couple of their researchers to Lexington to work with us. Initially, we focused on paving projects that had already been planned and approved. One was a heavily traveled street in downtown London, Kentucky, and the other was a rural road in Rockcastle County.

We eventually had fourteen sites that I managed around the state. All of the equipment used for the projects had to be thoroughly cleaned to assure that no foreign material remained. Then we received the coal tar at a certain temperature. I oversaw the paving operation for one mile of experimental material and then one mile of the regular material. After completing the paving I went back and walked the roadway, charting each significant blemish so that we would know it was already there and not caused by wear over time. This became my "on the job" management experience. I reported regularly to the people at the Koppers lab and received excellent guidance from them.

Governor Chandler wanted the project publicized across the state, and his office scheduled me to speak to civic clubs, especially in the eastern and western coal fields. I prepared a canned presentation that I became very familiar with after a period of time. I did one talk a week, especially during the mid-point of the project. The experience of standing up and speaking before those audiences helped me tremendously with public speaking going forward.

I remember giving a talk in February 1961 at a Kentucky Highway Conference held at UK during which I shared information about the experimental paving project I was supervising. Just as I began my talk the lights went out, which meant my slide projector also stopped working. The agenda was so full they would not wait for the electricity to come back on, so I gave my presentation without my slides. Another life lesson about being prepared and flexible.

Over the next several months we periodically checked on the project sites to evaluate how the roadway was holding up. We found the roads already beginning to deteriorate, primarily because of the extreme temperature variations in Kentucky, especially the cool fall/early-winter mornings followed by warmer afternoon temperatures. Ultimately, we could not adequately prove the materials useful on Kentucky roadways. However, it was used successfully in states like Arizona, which have a more stable climate.

The most significant event that occurred during my time with the highway department had nothing to do with the job. Meeting Gay Garred was the highlight of those two years. Gay attended UK and was from Morehead, Kentucky. While she was home for the summer, I would stop by and visit with her as often as I could as I traveled through eastern Kentucky with the highway project. When Gay returned to UK the following fall, we dated regularly. I am still not sure what she saw in me, but perhaps it was because I was older and owned a car. We became engaged during her junior year on Valentine's Day, 1960.

Gay and I were married in the Morehead Methodist Church on June 25, 1960. My father was my best man. I have never been more nervous than during my wedding, but somehow I made it through the day. There were two things about the wedding that I will never forget. First, it was a very, very hot day and the church had no air-conditioning. Second, I arrived at the church early in my casual clothes with a bunch of flowers. As I entered the church carrying the flowers, the people inside assumed I was the delivery guy.

We spent the first night of our honeymoon in a motel in Cincinnati. From there we drove to Washington, D.C., and then on to New York City. I had visited Washington on a school trip but Gay had never been there so we did the usual tourist things. However, Gay never let me forget that we spent one whole day of our honeymoon at Yankee Stadium watching a July 4 doubleheader.

When we returned to Lexington Gay continued working towards her college degree. Dr. Garred's only concern about our marriage was that Gay would not graduate from college. I promised him that Gay would complete her degree, which she did the year after we married. I vividly remember Gay's graduation because right after I left her to go find my seat she fainted. Her physician father came over to me and said, "She pregnant." My life was changing rapidly just as my highway department job, which paid $400 a month, was ending.

Just in time, an acquaintance in Maysville called me about a position at the Browning Manufacturing Company. I applied for the job, was hired, and began the company's training program in their mechanical engineering department. Initially, the move did not really address my desire to leave engineering, but it was something different and it also paid more than I had been making. All new managers in the company took the training program, which consisted of management training in the mornings and working in a particular area of the company in the afternoon: taking phone orders or working in different areas of the engineering department.

Only three weeks after moving to Maysville I was sitting at home on a Friday evening watching the local news on a Cincinnati station while Gay prepared dinner. Peter Grant, a veteran Cincinnati newscaster, came on and announced, "President John F. Kennedy has called up the Army Reserve. He believes that he must expand the US armed forces in reaction to the Russians building a wall between East and West Germany. This does not affect anyone in Ohio but this impacts our Kentucky neighbors significantly as the 100th Division in being called up." That is how I learned that my unit was being activated and assigned to Fort Pope near Alexandria, Louisiana.

The 100th Division drew reservists from Louisville, Lexington, and numerous small towns across Kentucky. Ironically, the unit did not include Maysville, but with everything going on in our lives I had not moved my assignment from Lexington to Maysville. Sitting there trying to process the news about returning to active duty, I recalled the stories I had heard about men called up for duty during World War II and not returning for six years. That first evening was tough as I contemplated what the immediate future might hold for Gay and me. As word spread through Maysville, many of our friends expressed how badly they felt for us. Other "friends" had some fun teasing me about how large the snakes were in Louisiana.

The unit captain asked me to report for duty immediately to get the unit prepared for active duty even though we were not required to report to Fort Pope for several weeks. Ironically, we were a transportation unit but had very few vehicles of our own because during our summer camps we borrowed vehicles from other military units. My first assignment was to go around the state and collect vehicles at various reserve units. We traveled by bus, dropping men off wherever there was a vehicle to pick up to be driven back to Lexington. We also brought maintenance people and parts with us because the vehicles were in terrible shape and many needed repairs.

Just a week before leaving for Fort Pope, we received new orders to report to Fort Chaffee, Arkansas. We placed all of our vehicles on a train bound for Arkansas and we followed soon thereafter. Initially, Gay decided not to follow me to Fort Chaffee because of her pregnancy. But as the time to leave drew closer, we decided that it would be better if she joined me. We knew several other families who were also going to Arkansas. Being called to active duty was even more difficult on some families. Those who owned and operated service stations or some other small business simply could not continue operating them during their absence. Many of these men, who were generally older and had served in World War II or Korea, had joined the reserves just for the extra income. In my case I joined the reserves simply to serve out my military requirement.

Upon arriving at Fort Chaffee we found a post in a state of disrepair. Twenty-nine hundred reservists would eventually arrive so it was essential that we get the water and sewage functioning in most of the buildings. We were never able to get the hospital up and running because weeds had grown up around and into the pipes, making it too expensive to repair. The barracks were very typical: four buildings and an orderly room. After the first month we were allowed to live off post, but with nearly three thousand soldiers and many of their families needing places to live, finding suitable housing became nearly impossible. Fortunately, a man who distributed Browning products in Fort Smith, Arkansas, found us a place. Our new "apartment" had been the storage room and bathroom in the rear of a plumbing shop. Still, we felt fortunate to have it.

I know Gay found the relocation very difficult but after she shed a few tears we just did what had to be done. But those types of experiences really helped to prepare Gay for the life of a corporate spouse. By necessity she became very independent and creative. For example, she taught herself to do repairs around the home better than I ever could. I did not even try to fix anything because I knew if it was going to be fixed correctly, then Gay was going to be the one who did it.

We found a doctor for Gay in Fort Smith as her pregnancy progressed. Like any young couple, we got a dog and began to make some friends. Don Crutcher, one of my college roommates, had been called up as well and we socialized with Don and his wife and played a lot of bridge. Don had become an officer but in a different section of the 100th Division so there was no conflict in our socializing.

The deployment in Arkansas would have been easier to deal with if we had known how long we would be there or where we might end up. I tried to focus on my work and we had gotten our number of vehicles in our unit up to 180. A transportation unit in those days was made up of 90 percent PFCs, a few sergeants, two lieutenants, and a captain. At summer camps I had worked in the orderly room and did various reports for the captain. He decided to put me in the orderly room to head dispatching as we were trying to take over supporting the rest of the 100th Division with vehicles while at camp. But an order came down at Fort Chaffee that a soldier must do whatever his MOS (military occupational specialty) stipulated within the organizational structure. I was the only spec-5 in our transportation division and a spec-5 was to drive two-star general Dillman Rash, who headed the division.

General Rash, a Louisville banker in civilian life, turned out to be a fine fellow. Sometimes he would tell me, "Tomorrow come with the jeep in your khakis." As ordered, I would pick him up wearing my khakis and we would go wherever he needed to be. Other times he might say, "At 10:00 you need to get your uniform on and take Mrs. Rash somewhere to make a speech." I soon figured out that the first thing the general did most mornings was to go to a quarter-mile track and run a couple of miles. We all exercised the best we could because we knew at some point we would be taking a physical exam. I finally asked the general if I could run between his start and completions times and he said yes. I would take my running shoes, pull off my shirt, and join him on the second lap. I knew he usually ran about eight laps so after seven I would drop off, get my stuff back together, and be standing at attention at the vehicle when he came running up.

While working for General Rash I had the opportunity to see President John Kennedy, who came to Fort Chaffee shortly after we were operational. I did not get to meet him, but I took General Rash over to meet the president and then followed along behind the car in which they rode. During his visit to the post President Kennedy gave an impressive speech. I will never forget that he told the hundreds of local businesspeople in the audience, "We will not close this base." But by the following August Fort Chaffee had closed.

I really enjoyed working for General Rash, but after a few weeks he told me I could not continue being his driver. Apparently the captains were complaining that the post was growing so rapidly that every soldier needed to be in his assigned job so the base could operate efficiently. So I left the general and returned to my dispatch work in the orderly room, where I had some interesting experiences, especially with the colonels. I was dispatching 180 vehicles but if the colonel's truck was not on time or a driver fell asleep or they did not drive right or any other problems arose, that came down on me. I managed two assistants, which turned out to be another good experience for me.

Since the captain had his hands full disciplining the soldiers and overseeing a multitude of administrative details, I dealt primarily with the lieutenant. Every day I would send off certain trucks to the same places. On any particular day, I might send 8 more vehicles to a different place. Also, we were not running 180 vehicles every day because of maintenance requirements. So one day the lieutenant came in and said, "You know, we've been here a good while and nearly everyone has served KP duty." I had served KP three times in basic so I was well aware of what it entailed. The lieutenant added, "I think you're going to have to go do that. Report to George Jenkins." I said, "Okay, Lieutenant." Then the conversation with Lieutenant Jenkins went like this:

Lieutenant: "I'll sit here in your place. By the way, what do you do here?"

Hardymon: "I dispatch these trucks, as you've seen us do."

Lieutenant: "Do you have a list of where they go?"

Hardymon: "No."

Lieutenant: "How do you know where they go?"

Hardymon: "I know sixteen go to ammo and eight go to here."

Lieutenant: "But you don't have it laid out?"

Hardymon: "No. I don't need to. I do it every day, week after week."

Lieutenant: "Well, Hardymon, forget about going on KP. Keep dispatching."

I will never forget that conversation with the lieutenant. I was not trying to make the work seem harder than it was; I simply did it the way that seemed most efficient for me.

Gay and I stayed at the base over Christmas and New Year's. From 1934 through Christmas 1999, I only missed Christmas with my mother one time. No matter where in the world I happened to be, I would get back to Maysville or she would come visit us. I do not know if that was love or self-discipline or some of both but whatever it was, that Christmas in Arkansas was the only one I missed spending with Mother.

The birth of one's first child is always a memorable experience. Gay was just shy of twenty-three years old when Jennifer was born, and neither of us was completely ready for what was about to happen. I carpooled from home to the base with several other soldiers and on the days that I drove, Gay was more or less homebound without a car. As the due date came and went, the guys in the carpool allowed me to skip my turns to drive until the baby was born. But one night I had to stay late at the base and the others had to leave without me. The base was about ten or fifteen miles outside Fort Smith and I called Gay to come get me. The next day Gay went into labor. I have always thought how fortunate we were that she had not begun labor the day before.

We rushed to the hospital, where Gay was assigned a room in which another woman was in labor as well. I found a chair in the corner of the room but I had to constantly keep moving to stay out of the way of the doctors and nurses. When Gay's delivery actually began they got me out of there quick because men were not permitted in the delivery room back then. I am not sure how long I waited, but eventually a nurse came out and told me that I was the father of a healthy baby girl. She then escorted me to a hallway where I could see Jennifer for the first time through a window to a room with all of the other newborns.

Anticipating a need for more living space, we had moved out of the tiny "storage room with a bath" and into a very small house that, fortunately, came with a window air-conditioner and a washer. As first-time parents we knew very little about caring for an infant and we had to learn a lot in a hurry.

Even though things were going relatively well for me, I think most of us were anxious to get out of the military and move on with our lives. Active military duty impacted our finances significantly. As a spec-5, I earned about 40 percent of what I would have been making in the private sector. But we managed to live on that income without any problems. We paid probably $30 to $40 monthly for rent and we even managed to save some money and never had to call upon our families for financial help.

Soldiers are often victims of their own rumors. Nobody started rumors better in the military than a transportation unit because we went all over the base and picked up any gossip out there. We would think we would be out by Mother's Day, then by Father's Day, and then by the Fourth of July, only to learn that was not to be. Since the tension between Russia and the US had not escalated further, we thought we might get out at any time. I found it difficult to think about life after the military until I was out. I finally completed my active duty in August 1962 but continued to report to Lexington monthly as required to fulfill my reserve obligation. The Cuban Missile Crisis that October kept the world on edge for thirteen days. I knew if hostilities erupted I would be back on active duty immediately. Fortunately, for me and for the world, that did not happen.

I did not realize that my absence caused a hardship for Browning Manufacturing as most of their employees worked on the manufacturing side and not in the engineering department. I had no correspondence with them while on active duty but I eventually learned they had filled my engineering position. Browning was committed to fulfilling their obligation to me, but I imagine they probably did not know where to put me because they had no idea when I would be back.

Returning to civilian life back in Kentucky began over fifty years of the most exciting time of my life. I experienced one business venture after another and one family event after another. But at the time, I could not have imagined what lay ahead of me as we were simply trying to restart our lives. Gay and I rented a house owned by the Hardymon businesses in the Valley View section of Maysville. The house sat only twenty yards from the railroad tracks running through Maysville. It was a very active rail line and when trains came roaring through the entire house shook. But after a while we hardly noticed. We were back home in Kentucky with our new daughter and our extended families near the river where my journey began. Life was good.

Chapter Two

Getting to Work

*I learned how to manage. People often say,
"He's a born leader." There is no such thing as
a born leader. Everyone gets help along the way,
sometimes a lot of help.*

Upon returning to Browning Manufacturing to restart my career, I learned that during my absence my position in engineering had been filled and that I was needed in the sales department. Of course, I had no sales experience and they did not tell me at that point if I might be relocated to one of the sales districts. Nevertheless, I attempted to take the news positively as might be expected of someone who needed a job. As it turned out, I spent only a short time back in Maysville as I finished my eight-week training program that had been cut short by military service. Browning engineers taught me how our products were designed and the workers in the factory showed me how the products were made.

By any measure, Browning made very mundane products that altered the horsepower in an electric motor to a different revolution, either higher or lower, to power various types of equipment. We sold v-belt sheaves and v-belts, roller chain sprockets, roller chains, and bearings as well as gear reducers and couplings. The product lines were available in a variety of sizes that could handle different horsepower and different torque. Through the training provided, I learned specific details about our products, such as the size of the screw that was holding it on the shaft, the size of the bore range, and how many teeth. Also, I kept a sheet of paper with all of the part numbers to help when needed. Fortunately, I was able to become familiar with the products rather quickly.

I began spending more and more time with the salespeople. Either the vice president of sales or the sales manager was usually in the office while the other was on the road working with our district managers. In addition to my in-house training, I spent time with two of Browning's senior people calling on distributors in places like Indianapolis, Atlanta, and Cincinnati. When I was finally told that Browning was sending me to Portland, I thought they meant Portland, Maine, but it was Portland, Oregon. When I told Mother and Dad I might as well have told them I was moving to Japan because to them Portland seemed a long way from home.

Browning only had about a dozen district managers at that time and they were assigned primarily to territories east of the Mississippi. Browning had two large territories out west, and a year earlier a salesperson had been transferred to cover California and Nevada. Browning utilized a master distributor system. The master distributor received a deeper discount so he could establish sub-distributors. Master distributors operated in Los Angeles, San Francisco, Portland, and Seattle. Sub-distributors were established in smaller places like Milton-Freewater, Oregon, or Yakima and Spokane, Washington. Sub-distributors made deals with the master distributor regarding how they would be compensated. I was sent to Oregon to establish additional distributors.

After learning I would be going to Portland, I spent part of my training period filling out cards about specific accounts in the region that were buying products and from whom they were buying them. The files contained people's names, addresses, and phone numbers. Card files seem rather primitive in today's digital world, but in the 1960s that was the most efficient way available to keep track of accounts.

On the first of November 1962, Gay and I set out on a cross-country car trip to our new home in Oregon. We took the southern route through Missouri to Colorado and then north. Before we left Boise at the foothills of the Olympic Mountains, we were told that we needed chains on our car if we expected to scale the snow-covered mountains that lay ahead of us. That turned out to be true.

Once in Portland we found a suitable apartment to rent and then Gay flew back to Kentucky. Browning vice president Frank Jones and I worked my new territory together for three weeks before Gay returned with Jennifer. Our small amount of furniture arrived in Portland before Gay returned and I hired some men to help me move it into the apartment. I provided the movers with six-packs of beer as incentive and under my supervision we managed to get most of the furniture in the wrong rooms. When Gay returned and saw the mess we had made she was not pleased.

One Saturday morning not long after settling into our apartment, the doorbell rang. As I approached the door I could see a man in uniform standing outside. I first thought was, "My God, the army is putting me back on active duty!" But when I opened the door the soldier simply handed me some papers that to my great relief turned out to be my discharge papers. I learned later that the military was attempting to cut expenses by shortening the required service of reservists like me. I was more than happy to help.

My northwest sales territory included Oregon, Washington, and parts of Idaho, Montana, and British Columbia and was divided into roughly a spoke pattern. Generally, I would drive out on a particular route making sales calls in seemingly every little town along the highway. Then I would return by a different route making sales calls. For example, I went south from Portland to Medford, Oregon, north to Vancouver, British Columbia, northeast to Spokane, and then southeast to Boise. At that time, it was accepted practice that a product, even a nonperishable product, would generally be sold within five hundred miles of where it had been made because of the costs of transportation. I realized that places like Atlanta, St. Louis, and Chicago would always generate more sales than my area in the Northwest. Nevertheless, learning and implementing Browning's sales philosophy gave me tremendous experience.

When not on the road making sales calls, I worked out of our apartment. I utilized my card files and I mailed postcards to alert distributors and other customers when I would be in their town. Browning discouraged us from making too many phone calls because, before cell phones, long-distance calls were very expensive. The master distributor and I would decide where we might go during a particular trip based on where I could provide the most help to him. Sometimes I would know the calls we were going to make in advance and other times I would not know until I arrived. It all depended on the sophistication of the master distributor's work.

Generally, I set out on Monday mornings with sample kits in my car. If the trip was out to Boise or Spokane, I would not return home until the following Friday evening. If I worked Portland, or even Eugene, I was generally able to return home that same evening. So two weeks out of the eight-week cycle I was able to spend most nights at home. I used my own car and the company reimbursed me for my mileage. But, averaging forty thousand miles annually, I wore out my old white Buick the first year. I eventually began flying out to Boise, especially when I had to go on out east into Idaho to Burley and Twin Falls or over to Missoula or Kalispell, Montana. I would fly to Spokane, rent a car, and make sales calls for a week. At the end of the week I would fly home for the weekend and then fly back to Spokane on the following Monday. I always tried to spend weekends at home unless I was attending a special event, such as a trade show in California.

While I was out on the road for Browning, there were definitely no three-martini lunches or entertaining clients in the evenings because my clients were mostly working people who had little time or inclination for such things. Occasionally, I might take a sawmill manager or the owner of a distribution firm out to lunch. After a full day of sales calls, I would return to my little roadside motel and fill out paperwork and prepare a call report.

When all of that was completed I became very familiar with what programs were on the three television networks. It never took long to determine the most comfortable little motel in a community and where I could find the best dinner options. I also learned that when I stayed in Aberdeen, Washington, I should always ask for a second-floor room because Aberdeen averages about 140 inches of rain annually.

I had a large territory to cover, but Browning's system proved to be an efficient way to cover it. However, everything about the process was very different from how sales and shipping are done today. Browning shipped their products by rail car so a rail car would be loaded in Maysville and shipped out to the distributors. For example, a rail car would go across the Southern Pacific and unload a portion in Los Angeles, then on up to San Francisco, Portland, and Seattle. That meant that when I took an order and the buyer asked when the product would arrive, the answer was always a little complicated. I might have to explain, "The rail car back in Kentucky is up to about twenty-five thousand pounds but it must weigh forty-five thousand pounds before it will be shipped. I don't know how our sales manager is doing in California in regard to filling the freight car so I'll have to let you know later." Of course, there were other options for delivering smaller items, like shipping them by bus, but that was much more expensive.

One of the most important aspects of my work in the Northwest, and one of the reasons I was promoted, was my success in establishing new distributors where there had not been any before. I would go into a town and talk to someone about my product line. Usually they already had some familiarity with Browning products because they had purchased them from a master distributor. As I established these new distributors, our orders grew significantly for a company doing only $9 or $10 million total sales per year. I worked on salary and received an annual commission that was similar to a bonus and based on a formula. I had a forecast of projected sales, and if I beat the forecast I received a certain amount for every dollar I came in over the forecast. My first year I just barely missed making $10,000, which motivated me to keep signing up distributors.

Gay and I absolutely loved living in Oregon, and our time there played an important role in our personal growth and development, much like our military experience had earlier. Moving across the country in 1962 made us more independent, and our one-year-old child had now lived in three states. We made some really good friends, most of whom were our neighbors in the apartment complex. Communication with the home office was difficult because of the time difference so I became much more self-reliant, which I really needed. By necessity, I had to make a lot of my own decisions. At the same time, Gay learned to operate on her own since I was away from home so often.

We usually returned to Kentucky twice a year, either for weddings or holidays, and I came back for Browning sales meetings. It always amused me that of all the salespeople coming into Maysville for the sales meetings, I was the only person actually from Maysville. Another odd aspect of returning for the sales meetings was that Browning required me to stay in a hotel, even though I could have easily stayed with Mother and Dad.

We thought—naively, as it turned out—that we were going to be in Oregon for the rest of our lives. We even began looking at possibly purchasing a lot out on Lake Oswego where we could build a house. Then one day I received a call from company headquarters informing me that a senior Browning family member, who had been number two in command at Browning, had died unexpectedly. A week later I received another call telling me that I was being transferred back to Maysville for a low-end administrative position. When one person moved up to take the deceased's position, everyone else in the organization moved up as well.

My new position, assistant sales manager, was at the bottom of that administrative pyramid. Back in Maysville I reported to the same two people I had trained under originally, Frank Jones, the vice president of sales, and Ed Smith, the sales manager. Frank had acquired additional responsibilities because of the senior person's death. Even though he still had sales reporting to him, he needed someone to spend time with the salespeople out in the field when he could not. I had a great mentor in Frank and a pretty fair boss in Ed.

I had built up the sales volume in the Northwest to the point that we divided the territory and hired two new salespeople. In those days it only took about $250,000 of sales to support a salesperson. Even after I had returned to Maysville, I spent a great deal of time back in the Northwest working with the new salespeople, and I eventually began going out there twice a year. The salespeople in Charlotte, Mobile, St. Louis, Louisville, and Indianapolis also reported to me.

I had seven direct reports so that meant that I would be away from home fourteen weeks a year with the salespeople and another two or three weeks at trade shows. My compensation continued to be based on how my territories did in comparison to the annual sales projections. No one outside the Browning family knew the company's profit because they did not have to tell anyone except their accountants and the auditors. So we knew what price we sold the product for but not how much profit it made.

As assistant sales manager, my life consisted of reviewing call reports of the salespeople, scheduling to go out with them, talking to some of their customers, and trying to take care of their business. Browning Manufacturing was very service oriented. I could be out at the Maysville Country Club's little nine-hole golf course on a Saturday and the loudspeaker would come on outside and someone would announce, "Hardymon, you're wanted on the phone!" I knew that meant I had a work-related phone call that I had to take care of immediately. It would often be someone in Seattle or San Diego who needed a part shipped out in a hurry. For emergency shipping we mostly used buses so I would go retrieve the part out of the warehouse, prepare a sales sheet, pack it, and take it down to the bus station. I needed no further reminding that I was the low person on the organization chart.

The plant began production each day at 7:00 a.m. when all of the machines were turned on. They drew such a surge of electrical power from Maysville's electric grid that Browning management asked the office staff not to come in until 7:30 a.m. to reduce the power surge. Most of the office staff left at 4:30 p.m., but because I had West Coast salespeople, I generally stayed until around 5:00 p.m. or later each day. We worked Monday through Friday and would usually go in on Saturday mornings for half a day.

Browning Manufacturing operated the factory in a very simple and yet interesting way that I was never able to replicate in any of my other management positions. The Browning in charge of the plant kept a chart behind his door on which he tracked the percentage of completed orders shipped. He ran the factory from 7:00 until 4:30 every day—eight and a half hours, with an hour off for lunch. When the plant reached 96 percent completed shipments, he cut back to an eight-hour day. But he would be sure to work half of the employees for five hours on Saturdays so that every employee worked every other Saturday. That way each employee would average forty-two and a half hours a week. When the complete order count dropped to 93 percent he brought everybody in on Saturday. It was a scheduling concept that worked great for Browning Manufacturing from 1936 to 1983 without a single employee layoff.

The manufacturing process mostly involved cutting metal. Workers made "teeth" for gears, bored out pieces for a shaft to go in, or assembled bearings. Most of the workers had grown up on farms surrounding Maysville and were good with their hands. The only problem was that some farmers simply could not adjust to highly structured work inside all day. There were occasional unsuccessful attempts to organize a union. As I reflect back on that time, most disruptions within the plant resulted from employees not being suited for that type of work, rather than how the plant was managed or how the employees were treated. I knew many of the workers at Browning personally because I had gone to high school with them.

As I had witnessed earlier in regard to the employees of my family's businesses, most of the Browning Manufacturing workers did not have checking accounts. Each Friday they took their paychecks either to the liquor store or the grocery to have them cashed. They gave their spouse a portion of the money and put the rest in their pocket. Most did not accumulate savings so they depended on the plant to be open each week so they could work and earn enough money to get through the next week. There were some women still working in the plant who had been hired during World War II because of the shortage of men workers. But there were not many new women hired during the time I worked at Browning.

I have wonderful memories of our time back in Maysville. Our son, Frank, was born and we bought our first house, which was very close to where I grew up. My parents enjoyed spending a lot of time with their grandchildren. Not much in Maysville had changed since my childhood, and the town looked the same. The doctors, lawyers, dentists, teachers, and coaches were the same ones I had admired in my youth. Maysville maintained the look, feel, and rhythm of a small rural town.

My greatest challenge during this chapter of my life was trying to balance work and my home life. My weeks on the road made that very difficult. Of course, Gay provided tremendous and unfailing support, not only during this time but throughout my career. We were truly partners in our life journey. It was also during this time that the church began to play a larger role in my life. Aunt Lillian influenced me greatly in regard to church, in large part because of the way she lived her life. It was easy to become involved in the church, civic activities, and local boards because I had graduated from high school as valedictorian, I had not caused much trouble as a youngster, and I had risen through the ranks with the town's largest employer without bragging about it. In addition to serving on the church board I also served on the local bank board and the board of the country club.

Browning Manufacturing encouraged my involvement in

the community. They also sent me to numerous seminars and financial schools for nonfinancial people where I learned about mergers and acquisitions, capital goods, and return on investments. For example, I attended the University of Virginia business school for two weeks and I attended numerous seminars and classes in Pittsburgh and other places.

It was very important for me to increase my financial knowledge and to broaden my understanding of business generally. I think Browning Manufacturing supported me in this because the Browning family was considering selling the company and knew that if they did so the three Browning sons would become very wealthy and were not likely to stay with the company. Also, Frank Jones, vice president for sales, kept mentioning my name when any opening came up. I did well financially with Browning Manufacturing and they put me in a position that would vault my career forward.

Rumors about the company being a good candidate for acquisition by another company were always swirling around. The company founder had died, as had another longtime family member who had helped run the firm. But there were still eight family members directly connected to the company, and they gave little indication of their intentions regarding the future. The Browning family remained the wealthiest citizens of Maysville. They were very frugal and did not squander their money. Still, they owned the largest homes in the nicest area and also owned ski lodges and homes in Florida.

In 1968 Emerson Electric, which is based in St. Louis, purchased Browning Manufacturing. It was not the biggest acquisition in the world, but it was $92 million at a time Browning Manufacturing was earning probably $30 million in revenue. One key reason it sold for that high a price was that the company had a number of utility bonds in it that were almost like cash. The purchase price of the company gave the rest of us, for the first time, some insight into the company's profits.

I was out in the Northwest doing sales calls when the news of the acquisition broke. I spoke with people back in Maysville and they tried to familiarize me with the conditions of the sale and what we could expect in regard to the consolidation. Of course, they told me, "There won't be any changes." But, without a doubt, this became the most disruptive period in my entire professional career. I completed my three weeks' work in the Northwest and did the best I could, even though I must admit my heart was not in it. I could not see how selling Browning Manufacturing could be a win-win for anybody, including me, other than the Browning family.

I knew absolutely nothing about Emerson Electric. For all I knew, it could have been a utility company. As the details of the sale became known over the next three months, Emerson shared some of their annual reports and began sending some of their people from St. Louis to Maysville to get up to speed on our company. Most of them seemed to have MBAs from Ivy League schools, and they were not much older than me. As it turned out, some of those people became life-long friends of mine.

Marvin Kolodzik had been hired by Browning away from an accounting firm before the Emerson deal became public. At the time we did not know why he had been brought in, but we thought he would strengthen our finance department. We learned later that he had been hired to help with financials in anticipation of the family selling the company.

Before the deal closed I learned that Emerson had chosen a few people, somewhere between five and ten, to whom they wanted to offer contracts. I nearly made what would have been the biggest mistake in my life. Emerson approached me two or three weeks before the close of the sale and asked me to sign a contract with them. I told them I did not want a contract, primarily because I had never had one with Browning. The contract they offered me was good in that it provided some security in case, for any reason, I was severed. The contract would have also spelled out my compensation package.

My primary concern with the contract presented to me was

that Emerson insisted on a non-compete clause that provided some assurance that I was going to stay with the company and not leave to work for a competitor. Over the years I came to appreciate that requirement more as I became involved in acquiring companies. But I did not appreciate it at the time. Emerson even flew me to St. Louis to discuss terms of the contract in more detail, but I still refused to sign a contract. In my mind I was not being difficult; I simply wanted to be left alone and see what transpired.

When I returned to Maysville from St. Louis, one of Browning's senior managers told me emphatically, "Jim, Emerson is not going to close this deal unless you guys sign the contracts." I had not talked with anyone else about their position regarding a contract. But my mentor Frank Jones's body language told me that he did not want a contract either. Going through the contract discussions had a lasting impact on me. It was not a momentous or even a big decision on my part, but I made it big. Eventually, I signed and moved on.

The new owners wanted Browning Manufacturing to begin doing four things that they had not done previously. First, they wanted Browning to diversify out of Maysville. Second, they wanted to look at new acquisitions. Browning had always taken the position that if something was not created in Maysville it was not worth having. Third, they wanted to see more innovation and new products. We made a lot of v-belt sheaves and roller chain sprockets, products that would not be considered a gateway to innovation or creativity, considering that the manufacturing process had not changed in decades. Even Leonardo da Vinci made roller chains out of wood that conveyed motion from one place to another with a chain. And fourth, Emerson wanted to open an international market. Browning Manufacturing had just one person outside the United States to cover sales worldwide.

I have always thought that Larry Browning, who became president of the division after the death of his uncle, promoted me to the Emerson people. I valued his support because with all the changes and new people coming in, I felt that I had to prove my value to the company all over again. When Emerson decided to put the initiative for new products and innovation under one person, they moved me out of sales and gave me the title of new product manager, by far the absolute worst job title I ever had. The move took me out of my security blanket in sales and put me into a position whose job duties none of the other six hundred Browning employees even understood. I believe Emerson chose me for the position because they wanted someone internal and Larry Browning likely recommended me. Larry and Emerson were putting a lot of faith in a young man who did not even possess a passport.

I had benefited tremendously from my two years of work experience in Oregon. Additionally, I had traveled the country with our salespeople and had set up trade shows in New York and other locations, which gave me valuable experience working with union employees. The other two or three people in the company with similar experience were all older and more established in their current positions and would have been more difficult to replace. My position as assistant sales manager was not exactly the most important job in the company, so it was not that difficult to choose another district manager to promote to my previous position.

My ascension to new product manager came with a salary increase and even warranted an article in the *Maysville Ledger Independent.* Initially, I was told to look for items that Browning could buy out and place those products under our brand name. I also watched for new materials that could be used in our manufacturing processes beyond cast iron and steel. I also discovered some gadgets we could buy that would control the torque and speed of a motor.

Two of the people who had come from Emerson to assess the Maysville operation passed along suggestions to me for possible acquisitions. They reported to the president of Emerson and were always on the lookout for new acquisitions and their suggestions proved very helpful. I began visiting the companies I found or that they suggested, and we started buying their products aggressively.

I obtained a passport, which proved essential since Emerson wanted to expand international sales. Every unit within the company was required to have someone involved with international operations, and that group began holding regular meetings. It was not long before I made a three-week trip to Europe, which was my first experience outside the United States except for Canada. I flew to London and then traveled to northern England to visit a Goodyear plant that supplied us parts and where I was received well. Once I moved on to Paris, communication became a little more difficult. I found that even if the people I needed to work with at the factories spoke English, they would only speak French to me. They seemed to really enjoy watching me struggle through the language barrier. After Paris, I went on to Brussels, Munich, Stuttgart, and Frankfurt. At each destination I never ventured too far out of the urban centers.

One of the biggest changes under Emerson's ownership was diversifying the location of the company. The distribution center was the easiest segment of Browning Manufacturing to move. We built a 175,000-square-foot building that included a chain in the floor that allowed workers to pull the cart off at a station, check the paperwork, put a product in, and then send it on to the next station. We went from tracking a product by part number to tracking it by bin number, which dramatically improved the efficiency of the center. In November 1970, we relocated the distribution center to Eaton, Ohio, 125 miles northwest of Maysville. The entire move took only four days.

One Friday later that month I was asked to stay at the office a bit longer. The office had cleared out, but a meeting was still under way behind closed doors. I sat at my desk, waiting. Finally one of the Browning family members left the meeting, slamming the door behind him. He walked right by me without saying a word or even acknowledging my presence, and rushed out of the building.

He had been told in the meeting that responsibility for the distribution center was being taken from him. Then someone came out of the meeting and asked me to join them. They told me I would take over the distribution center, which meant that I was going from managing eight people to administering an operation of two hundred employees.

My immediate and most crucial task was to find workers for the new distribution center. We needed as many people as we could hire as quickly as possible. I learned that Parker Hannifin Corporation, which operated a plant near our new distribution center, planned a long Christmas layoff and might even let some employees go permanently. I met with their plant managers and we were able to hire many of their furloughed employees, which helped get us through a crucial time.

The distribution center worked two twelve-hour shifts, and I stayed in a nearby motel until it was running smoothly, meaning we shipped all of the back orders and they were mostly correct. Then, for a time, I traveled back and forth between Maysville and the distribution center, staying there two or three days a week. Of course, I had never run a distribution center before but I received a lot of help from some of the senior people. I knew the product and I could answer many of the questions from the workers as to where something belonged. We did not transfer any people to Ohio except the manager, so everyone was pretty green and sometimes mistakes were made. When that happened I was not the type of person who jumps up and down and cusses somebody out if they did something wrong. I tried to get along with everyone and in the process I learned how to manage. People often say, "He's a born leader." There is no such thing as a born leader. Everyone gets help along the way, sometimes a lot of help.

After a time I got a call from St. Louis that Vince Gorguze, president of Emerson Electric, was coming to the distribution center to meet with me. I had no idea what to expect, but I assumed that Emerson planned to put their own person into my position. Gorguze flew into a nearby small airport in Richmond,

Indiana, on a King Air—which, as far as I was concerned, could have been a 747. It was a biggest private plane I had ever seen.

I drove Gorguze straight to the distribution center, where he walked through the facility shaking hands and speaking to everyone. He asked a lot of informational type questions. After returning him to the airport, we got out of the car and he said, "Looks like you guys are doing everything you can." We shook hands and he got back on his plane and left. His short visit made a lasting impression on me.

My experiences with a large company during this time helped me to begin placing my work in a broader context and I began thinking about bigger ideas. One thing I had learned for certain: I much preferred operations over sales. I like the challenges of efficiency, throughput, containing costs, and getting the work done. I learned the importance of process and the necessity of getting workers to buy into the process and to understand it, even if I rotated them from one job to another. I derive tremendous satisfaction from completing jobs and looking over the numbers at the end of each month. I wanted to know how much we shipped, how much was on time, how much we spent, how much overtime we used, and how many temporary employees were necessary. I constantly explored every facet of the operation so it could be improved.

I began taking a larger role in the acquisitions side after the distribution center became firmly established. We bought a company near Munich and we also bought Van Gorp in Iowa. The Van Gorp purchase took quite a bit of time and it reported to me after we bought it. Around the same time, Larry Browning moved to Emerson and his brother Bob took over as president of Browning Manufacturing. The dominoes started falling again and I was made executive vice president. Engineering began reporting to me but sales still reported directly to the president of the division.

A little over a year after my promotion, Emerson began talking with me about other opportunities. Allan Gilbert, who reported to the Emerson CEO and oversaw the company's organizational strength and succession planning, came to Maysville and sat at our dining room table talking well into the evening. It turned out that his only reason for coming was to see if I would ever be willing to leave Maysville, even though he never asked me directly. He learned during his visit that my parents still lived there, my children were in the local school, I was very active in the community, and I was well established in the town. But during our conversation that evening, Gilbert talked about an open position within Emerson—although he never even hinted that it was a position for which I might be considered.

Sometimes during business trips to Emerson headquarters in St. Louis I would learn about a division presidency that had opened. I understood that Emerson normally tried to find some high-ranking official either in that division or another one to fill the job. Therefore, because of my current ranking within the company, I knew I was not going to get that one. Thinking we would be in Maysville for at least a few more years, Gay and I found a house we liked and purchased it.

Only three months after closing on our new home, I learned about an opportunity for me in St. Louis. Perhaps I could have told them I was not interested, but then I may never have gotten another opportunity in the future. Emerson was a midwestern company and much different from what one finds on the East Coast. East Coast people drive by twelve or fourteen businesses every day during their commute that would likely have positions that would be promotions for them. But in smaller urban areas like St. Louis, those types of positions were not as abundant, so people tended to stay with the company longer. Also, Emerson placed a great deal of emphasis on loyalty.

As it turned out, we had nearly a year to consider what we wanted to do as Emerson did not move very quickly on the offer. It really never became a question of not doing it because at that point Gay and the children were ready to move. My son would have enthusiastically supported moving to any place that had a

McDonalds. But a move was a much more difficult prospect for Mother and Dad. They were very close to the grandchildren and were our primary babysitters. And, like most grandparents, they did everything they could to spoil Jennifer and Frank.

Before the move, Vince Gorguze took the time to offer me good advice regarding living in St. Louis. As is true of most large cities, an interstate highway circled the core of St. Louis, and the cost of property inside that circle was higher than outside. We also knew that suburban St. Louis schools would be very different from those in Maysville. Gay began searching for a new house—our tenth since we were married—focusing primarily on the far west side of St. Louis outside I-270. She finally zeroed in on a neighborhood that she thought would be best for our children.

With home issues under some control, I turned my attention even more to my new position. Particular jobs within the corporate world can be very satisfying, and one of those is being president of a division. A division president still has bosses to report to, either within the company or externally, like a board or shareholders. But you have direct responsibility for operations, sales, human resources, and generally a legal office. It was a position I was eager to try. I really believed that I was ready for the St. Louis move even though I was going into a totally new environment. I left the manufacturing and product area without knowing anybody in my new division.

Emerson Electric had been founded in St. Louis, where the corporate headquarters remained along with one manufacturing division that produced defense products. Emerson's St. Louis campus was located about seven miles out of the city center while the rest of the company's manufacturing was located elsewhere. Emerson began making electric motors and eventually began putting the motors into different types of machinery like radial arm saws, table saws, and bench saws. But these types of machine tools required a more powerful motor than a portable electric tool. So Emerson bought a company that had designed woodworking tools and folded it into the motor division. When it grew large enough to become its own division, they could not think of a better name for it than Special Products Division.

Arriving for work at Emerson that first day, I introduced myself to the receptionist in Emerson's outer office. She called for Linda Wojciechowski, who would be my administrative assistant, to come out immediately. My first impression was that she was very polite and stood a head taller than me. Knowing that I was coming, she had already assembled the division leaders in a conference room. I can only imagine that when I first walked into the room they looked me over and thought, "Who's this young guy?" Even at first glance they knew that my predecessor was a more seasoned manager. Moreover, I was the first division president at Emerson to come from an industry unknown to them.

The Special Products Division was unique in that we had a contract to sell our products exclusively to Sears and Roebuck Company under the Craftsman brand. The contract stipulated that we would take Sears' forecast for the next year and come up with our cost base. The markup was set by the contract so they could audit our costs or do whatever they wanted to and then we could start production. During the years I was there, we overran their forecasts. When that occurred, we made more profit, which we split with Sears. We sent them a check at the end of the year, but if we had ever come in under the forecast we would have absorbed the loss. Fortunately, that never happened. The Special Products Division had a major manufacturing facility in Paris, Tennessee, about two hours from Memphis. Subsequently, we added a new plant in Murphy, North Carolina.

During my time in St. Louis I benefited immensely from the very best mentor anybody could ever hope for, Charles "Chuck" Knight, Emerson's CEO. Our relationship began back in Maysville when Chuck came in as a consultant after Emerson bought Browning. Somehow he just picked me out of the pack. He was always making some individual contact with me even though he did not become my direct boss until later. My immediate supervisor during my time in St. Louis was Vince Gorguze. I am sure he knew I had a direct line to the CEO, but I do not think it ever concerned him since I was president of one of the smaller divisions.

Chuck liked sports and we began attending a few University of Kentucky basketball games together in Lexington. Even though we enjoyed one another's company and going to events together, our relationship never became what one might call buddy-buddy but instead continued as more of a mentoring relationship. With the exception of my parents and the support of Gay and my children, Chuck became the most important person in my rise up the corporate ladder.

Chuck thought very strategically and his decisions were usually right. He could be very tough and was outspoken to the point that I often became very angry with him and wanted to prove him wrong about something. Chuck was not shy about pointing out a person's shortcomings and I vividly remember two specific criticisms he directed at me. Once Chuck told me, "You know the one thing about you that you really need to get over? If we are discussing ten items and on number seven we disagree, you're not worth anything on eight, nine and ten." Another time he told me, "Jim, sometimes you try to make decisions too quickly and just forge ahead. That might work for you most of the time, but when it does not work, it can lead to some really bad mistakes."

Once I really challenged Chuck regarding something very simple, but I am certain he never forgot it. Chuck had a tendency to use some rather vulgar words that affected people differently. But that did not bother me as much as him occasionally calling me dumb. About the twelfth time he did that over a period of years I finally told him, "Chuck, I want you to know that when you call me dumb it makes me very angry. I lose all concentration on what we are doing, I lose faith in you, and I lose faith in the issue we are working on. You must stop calling me that." He did not respond but he never called me dumb again. It might seem odd, but I considered that exchange a very important breakthrough in my career.

As in any business situation, my direct reports were crucial to our division's success. The finance area was extremely important because of the type of contract we had with Sears. We had to manage not only to Emerson's desires for financial information but also report to Sears. Mike Evans handled our financial affairs and Ernie Lovelady oversaw sales while Charlie Ray handled operations. We received assistance from outside our division for human resources support and legal advice. JoAnn Harmon Arnold in human resources was especially helpful. She had joined Emerson as a temporary secretary in 1966 and eventually worked her way up to become the company's first female executive in 1980. The Emerson legal office assisted whenever we established a new manufacturing site. The selection of a location and negotiating with state officials was always handled centrally by the corporate office.

Our management team worked well together, considering Ernie Lovelady expected to be named the division president before I got the position. I assumed that the people around Ernie supported him because I went in as a complete unknown from the outside. But in a situation like the one I inherited, I knew I could not let that worry me. I had to assume the people who put me in the position knew what they were doing and at least thought I had the background to be successful. I tried very hard to integrate myself into the existing Emerson culture. I did not try to break out of the mold, as some new managers mistakenly do. I was in the office from 8 or 9 to 5, whatever was required, and I did not skip out in the middle of the afternoon to play golf because I knew I had to work as hard as I expected my team to work. I also got to know my managers and their families outside of the workplace through a variety of social events.

I visited the manufacturing plants often because I always preferred going to the other person's operation instead of telling someone to come to me. I would sometimes take the company plane to site visits. We leased a plane that was headquartered in Paris, Tennessee. I would try to plan my trip for when someone from Paris was coming to St. Louis and then I would fly back with them. Or I could fly commercially into Memphis and someone would pick me up and drive me to Paris.

In 1978 we began manufacturing our first product line in Taiwan and the initiative went well. Because of that initiative I am sometimes accused of starting the outsourcing of American manufacturing. While I am unaware of who outsourced their manufacturing first, I am sure it was not me. It might have been Sears because they told us, "You've got to make our drill press somewhere else." So we found a partner that happened to be in Tai Chung, Taiwan.

Ernie Lovelady, who oversaw our sales to Sears, went to Taiwan to get the operation started and I followed sometime later. One of our big concerns at the time was that the people working for us in Taiwan might give all our proprietary information to a relative or friend down the street who would then begin making drill presses and selling them out of the back of a truck. But the Taiwan initiative worked out well and it became another great learning experience for me. We sold exclusively to Sears and we engineered the product in conjunction with their marketing people, as we did not have marketing people per se. Even though we had people who spoke Chinese, we did not produce sales catalogs.

Emerson bought the machinery and Sears bought the tooling. We bought a standard piece of machinery that would cut a round object and put a bore in it or thread it or whatever was needed. We were responsible for making sure we bought the right machinery. Of course, there was always the fear that the contract might be cancelled any given year. We generated up to $100 million of annual business with Sears while I was there. It was only $40 million when I arrived, but I will not take the credit for the increase. We only did what Sears told us to do because we did not sell the product. Sears simply blew the volume up.

Our biggest challenge became getting the finished product out the door. Sears had what was called a "blue Monday," which to my knowledge not many other companies had. Other companies would tell you what week they were going to ship the product, but it did not always ship that week. With Sears, if the product was not shipped on time we had to report it on Monday morning and say what we were going to do about it. This made one very conscious of on-time delivery.

I considered Sears a great company during my close association with them between 1976 and 1979. They graded you on four things: price, on-time delivery, quality, and innovation. By focusing on those core values, they educated suppliers about their importance and caused them to think about something outside their own backyard. It was a really great system, and to this day I am not exactly sure how Sears eventually lost their way. I suppose too many other people got into the business. Nevertheless, I had a good run with Sears.

Chapter Three

Climbing the Corporate Ladder

*We were up against a bad wind
and the way the orders stopped arriving,
one would have thought that the mailman had been shot.*

Something always seemed to come up at Emerson over the Christmas holidays that would require my attention. Around Christmas 1978, while attending a holiday party in Chicago, Chuck Knight struck up conversations with several people who owned about 25 percent of SKIL Power Tools, which traded on the New York Stock Exchange. Subsequently, Chuck called three of us into his office on Christmas Eve morning. The family and I had planned to leave that day to travel to Maysville but we had to postpone our departure until I could get away. Chuck's conversation with the SKIL people had convinced him they were ready to throw their stock into an arrangement in order to sell SKIL. My colleagues and I argued against the idea because we did not consider SKIL to be a very solid company or very well managed. Chuck decided to buy SKIL anyway. Emerson and SKIL agreed that Emerson would acquire over 50 percent of the SKIL capital stock.

Chuck and I attended a University of Kentucky basketball game in Lexington on January 20, 1979, and unfortunately, UK lost to Tennessee 55-66. On the way back to St. Louis Chuck told me, "The day we acquire SKIL Power Tools you will be named president of the company." I thought at the time he might be over-promoting me, but I felt confident as my time at Browning and Emerson had gone relatively smoothly. But to be successful and move up you have to have something to reach for. So, after cruising along and still only forty-four years old, I suddenly found myself head of an international manufacturing and supply company. SKIL was the largest acquisition Chuck had made at that point, and it seemed to be a rather risky one. SKIL Power Tools had made less than $1 million the previous year and it only accomplished that level of profit by dressing up the company in preparation for the sale.

SKIL stock closed on the New York Stock Exchange on the morning of March 23, the day of the sale. At 9:30 a.m., I received a telephone call that an airplane was waiting to take me to Chicago. After arriving in Chicago, I met SKIL's major owners and Chuck Knight for lunch. Afterward, I went to the SKIL office by myself and immediately called a staff meeting where I announced that the CEO of SKIL would be stepping down but would maintain an office in the building. Emerson had never acquired anything where they changed leaders the very first day. John Sullivan, son of the company's founder, had been chairman and CEO of the standalone company, and had supported the sell-off from day one. After the acquisition, Sullivan become a member of the Emerson Board of Directors.

I inherited a very senior management team at SKIL that over time had become stale and too set in their ways. I remember meeting their chief legal counsel, who we knew would not be needed because all legal matters would be handled by our corporate office, the president, a human resources person who provided tremendous support, and a chief operating person who turned out to be very good at his job. Early on it was difficult to tell how good the operations person really was because he had very little money to work with and was trying to get by with almost nothing. With the exception of the president, who actually ran the company under the CEO, the management team all pitched in and tried to adjust. I am sure I looked awfully young to them probably because I was awfully young.

I recall Saturday mornings standing at the window in my office at SKIL overlooking Edens Expressway and thinking, "I don't know. I don't know if I'm going to make this one or not." It was a tough challenge and the high interest rates at that time didn't make it any easier. We were up against a bad wind and the way the orders stopped arriving, one would have thought the mailman had been shot. Operating within a national economic downturn, I had to get my hands around an operation that had plants in Skokie and Wheeling, Illinois, two locations in Arkansas, as well as plants in Canada, Australia, Europe, and Venezuela. I began having two or three conversations a day with Chuck Knight to work my way through this economic downturn.

Between January 6 and March 23, 1979, the day the sale closed, I set out to learn the company as rapidly as was feasible. I made unannounced visits to some of the company's locations, attended conventions pertinent to our product line, reviewed annual reports and any other documents that had been gathered during the acquisition process. Everything confirmed my first impression that SKIL was a weak company. Nevertheless, we thought we could buy better raw materials, improve transportation of the product, and put in place a better compensation program, and significantly restructure factory programs. In the corporate world, the saying goes that if you need to change a company 30 percent, you must start over rather than try to implement changes piecemeal by whittling away at the organization.

We promised the Emerson shareholders we would make SKIL a 10 percent pre-tax company. This pre-tax percentage would not dilute Emerson's overall financials to a great degree. We calculated at the time of the purchase we needed roughly $20 million additional profit to equal Emerson's pre-tax profit percentage, not of revenue. We put our heads down and just kept working, and fortunately the economy began to improve by 1982. We closed SKIL operations in Australia and Canada and moved to Mexico. We made management changes in Europe because that was our most profitable region and we wanted to maximize volume there.

I knew Emerson never settled for "good enough." If a business opportunity arose and I was not fulfilling it, I was just as subject to criticism as somebody doing a really bad job. If this happened, Emerson would start counseling you about what might need to be done differently. I knew I had to find a way to explain to corporate why I was not making the necessary changes to capitalize on those opportunities.

The former president of SKIL left the company within six months. We had a person running our European company who could have been cast as a German soldier in a World War II movie. He was very difficult to manage. I worked it out so he would have to attend meetings in the States five times a year and I would go to Europe seven times a year. Since Europe was our most profitable area and it should have been doing even better, I decided to try to work with the person already there.

Emerson required that the entire management team of all of its companies meet with the corporate officers once a year in what was basically a day and a half meeting. The team and I would come to St. Louis early that morning to get ourselves organized. Then the corporate officers would join us for lunch, after which we'd conduct the actual meeting. We presented an overview of our company and reviewed our strategic plan, financials, and needs. We concluded the presentation with our five-year forecast.

We were in the final stages of one of our meetings when the European manager got up to make his presentation. It sounded like the same presentation he had made five times before after which nothing happened. Every time somebody questioned him he rose up with a rebuttal. Finally he said, "You know, I've got to go. I've got a plane to catch." He gathered up his material and briefcase and walked out of the room. Chuck Knight looked at me and said, "Fire that arrogant son of a bitch." The person knew what was coming, I suppose, and decided to go out on his own terms by making a dramatic exit.

I moved quickly to build a strong team and in the middle of all of this Chuck assigned me three more divisions. Now the chainsaw, ceiling fan, and the string-line trimmer divisions all reported to me. This change caused me to act quickly to build management staffs in those areas. I brought in Bill Davis, whose father had at one time served as president of Emerson, to work in my division in St. Louis just as a way to get him started in Emerson. At that point Bill had already built a successful career and over time we became great friends. I also brought in Ernie Lovelady, a great marketing and salesperson, and George Sherman to add to the SKIL Chicago team. Sherman always reminded me of the basketball player who would make a mistake on one end of the court but before you could find a substitute for him he would make something terrific happen at the other end of the court. Once I became used to how he worked everything was fine. Sherman began running operations in the United States while I kept running the rest of the worldwide operation, particularly Europe. So, with Chuck's help, I built a solid team who stuck with me and provided the talent and hard work we needed to succeed. Bill Davis would later become the CEO of R. R. Donnelley, and George Sherman became the CEO of Danaher.

My experience with SKIL provided me with a real challenge, but I never had any doubts about my ability to manage a business. Much of my time managing SKIL occurred during the Jimmy Carter administration, when all of industry felt the challenges of a poor economy, gasoline shortages, and extremely high interest rates. I tried never to take my work concerns home, but of course Gay could tell if something was weighing on my mind. Still, we seldom discussed work issues. I had faith that if a particular assignment did not work out, Emerson would find another position for me. I was loyal, I trusted management, and management trusted me. I always tried to keep my ego in check through all of my various positions so that if something did not work out it would not have been devastating. Of course, some times were more difficult than others. On the rare occasions I did feel pressure, it was mostly pressure I had brought on myself.

SKIL began selling to Home Depot when they were still a

small operation and to Walmart during the time Walmart still operated mostly in small markets outside major metropolitan areas. George Sherman and Ernie Lovelady convinced me we had to do more supplying outside the country. We were already a little ahead of our time because we had begun buying product primarily from Taiwan, not China. Wherever we purchased materials we also sold our product there. Outside the United States we sold through smaller hardware stores rather than the big box stores.

We were very dependent on our own sales and marketing department. SKIL had its own sales department, and the employees in the foreign areas reported to me. Many companies sell through agents and dealers, but we had our own people out selling our product. It was very expensive way to operate, but it allowed us to penetrate areas where sales were weak. For example, if you do not have your own people in California it is very hard to go to California and set up a third party to sell your product and do it well. It is important to get one's own people selling there on the ground.

The move from St. Louis to Chicago impacted our family life tremendously. Chicago was the most difficult of all of our family moves. I was extremely busy and traveling all the time. Again, Gay found and bought our house, this one in Lake Forest. That house turned out to be a great place to live. It was the only house we ever purchased that I did not see beforehand. Gay simply could not wait on me to see the house, and I had great faith in her judgment.

I almost lost my daughter's love and respect after we moved to Chicago. The move happened between Jennifer's junior and senior year of high school. Moving children becomes harder as they grow older, and moving during their high school years has to be the worst. Jennifer continued to do well in school, but she just was not happy. In St. Louis she had been involved in all types of school activities and in leadership roles, but by the time she enrolled in her new high school all of those slots had been filled. Fortunately, she did something that might have been prompted by her inheritance of my genes: she got a part-time job working in a Gap clothing store. When in doubt, go to work.

During my first year in Chicago, I worked really hard for very long hours, leaving me little time to do things outside of work. I traveled back and forth to St. Louis so much the company purchased a plane for our use. I was not working closely with our corporate analysts at that point, but I suspect they were questioning our decision and wondering if we made the right acquisition at the right time. SKIL was sixth in market share worldwide and that was not a good place to be in to succeed. The market challenges did not deter Emerson from pushing forward because the company had money, a track record of success, and multiple divisions. Along with SKIL, Emerson purchased Western Forge, a hand tool company in Colorado Springs, Weed Eater, Beaird-Poulan Chainsaws, and Ridge Tool, which manufactured pipe wrenches and plumbing devices like threaders. All of these companies were placed under my supervision along with the Special Products Division, which was a pretty heavy load. Fortunately, they were all managed well.

Black and Decker, our number one competitor, was way ahead of us in regard to portable electric tools, in part because their tools were a little heavier than ours. We also competed against Bosch, Ryobi, and Milwaukee Tool, who outsold us as well. Milwaukee Tool made a good construction person's tool. At the same time the Japanese were expanding their exports in this area, adding still more competition. But offering a wide variety of tools was SKILs primary strength. Big box stores prefer a company that offers an entire line of hand tools rather than just one or two that get placed on a shelf by themselves. This was just the leverage we needed to improve our overall sales volume. Early on, True Value Hardware stores became one of our largest buyers. We were unable to get our product into the Sears stores because they had contract suppliers that provided tools manufactured under the Craftsman name and that met their hand tool needs.

Most consumers who needed to purchase a tool to fix something around the house were very familiar with the Black and Decker brand. To compete with Black and Decker at a lower consumer price point, a company had to be large enough so the cost could be spread across the organization to get to a level where a particular product could still be sold for a lower price regardless of the profit on that product.

Chuck Knight and I discussed these types of strategies often. We bought Beaird-Poulan and he said, "What are you going to do?" I replied, "Well, Homelite, a Textron company, is the one that is giving us the most trouble." Chuck interjected, "Yes, and you know they have their own sales force and they are nationwide, whereas we are more focused on the Southeast. It will take you forever to challenge their market share. You've got to find a workable strategy. For example, make a chainsaw for $99 that you can sell for $99 and go to Sears. Then you'll have the sales force, you'll have the national market. But first you've got to get a chainsaw."

So we took a Weed Eater electric motor and put it on a chainsaw. By this time President Gerald Ford began warning the nation that the United States would implement measures to decrease the purchase of foreign oil and that Americans better get some wood stored away because they might need it. So people purchased chainsaws and hung them in their garages, even if they never used them. We were able to make an electric chainsaw that sold at the price point we needed so that consumers could afford it. We decided this would be a unique product because we could not have produced an entire product line in that manner that would have sold to commercial chainsaw users. But we kept selling those large Woodsman professional chainsaws, particularly in the Southeast.

The first big change we made in the SKIL tool product line was to utilize plastic, a change our competitors were also trying to make. We conducted view tests to judge consumer reaction to the change to plastic. We would invite fifteen people to come in and sit and talk to our people about this new device. We had a wall that had one-way glass you could see through and we could also hear their conversations. I remember they kept referring to the plastic that had been introduced into the product as "Mickey Mouse!" Consumers were more familiar with using a cast iron product that weighed substantially more. They identified the weight of the product with better quality.

But the move to using more plastic rather than cast iron proved to be the breakthrough we needed to begin selling to True Value and Home Depot. Those stores liked our product because it was unique and could be sold at a price that competed with the big boys in the hand tool market. To compete, SKIL had to maintain quality, reduce our manufacturing costs, and sell our product at a competitive price. We also had to move out of Chicago, where we had a tough union situation. That transition created some bumps in the road as we relocated manufacturing to Walnut Ridge and Heber Springs, Arkansas, and then to Mexico.

Innovation remained the key to our success. For example, George Sherman and his team came up with a battery-operated screwdriver. The product was assembled in Mexico, where we could train somebody in fifteen minutes. We offered it for a price as low as any electric screwdriver on the market. It became the lead tool that our salespeople used to get in the door. After talking about the screwdriver, the salespeople would quickly add, "Now, you do know our company is really well known for our quarter horsepower circular saws." If we could get in the door selling a new battery-operated screwdriver, then we could bring in the circular saw because they wanted it anyway, but they did not want it by itself.

My time at SKIL always reminds me of a funny story about my dad. In spite of all of his wisdom, honesty, and hard work, he never really understood what I was doing with my life and career until I went to SKIL. He knew something about portable electric tools. When I visited Dad in Florida we often took walks together. On one of our walks we went by a house under construction and Dad wanted to stop in and talk to the builder. I later learned the builder expected him because he generally stopped by every day to talk. On this visit Dad saw a SKIL portable electric tool nearby and pointed to it and asked the builder, "What do you think about that tool?" The guy said, "Oh, it's all right, I guess, but it's not what it used to be." Dad responded, "Well, then you should talk to this kid here. He's president of SKIL." That story describes the essence of my dad when you got right down to it.

The success my areas were experiencing meant I became eligible for a $1 million bonus promised by Chuck Knight. I was pleased to receive the bonus but learned that the award came in Emerson stock rather than cash. In addition, I was not allowed to sell my Emerson stock, which meant that I had to pay taxes on it. I still own Emerson stock because in the long run getting stock was actually better than receiving cash. My financial situation continued to improve over time, but as my salary increased our family's lifestyle remained virtually unchanged. Jennifer and Frank had no interest in going to really expensive schools. Jennifer attended the University of Missouri and Frank went to the University of Kentucky, so even sending our children to college was not a huge expense. As time went on and I received larger bonuses, I was able to save most of the money I made.

I continued to work hard and long hours, but I did begin taking note of my health. I knew I was not getting enough exercise and my cholesterol count began heading in the wrong direction. I tried running but did not care for that. I also tried biking but the weather in Chicago is so uncertain and frankly, I did not think riding a bike in sleet, snow, and a cold wind worked for me. So I purchased exercise equipment and worked out at home. I began with a stationary bike, then added a treadmill and, over time, other equipment to an exercise room. After a couple of years exercising became a regular part of my life, as it still is today.

Chuck had continued putting other divisions under me as the company had evolved, and I began unofficially reporting to him. The other segment leaders may have had more volume than I did and maybe more companies, but we were doing somewhat the same thing and it was kind of an interesting situation. It was like the difference between being chairman of the board and the chief executive officer. I went to St. Louis for the meetings in which the division leaders talked for a day and a half. But Chuck did not want to argue with me about anything. He told me, "You stay out of this. Let the others talk." So I was on my way to the executive vice president position—whether I wanted it or not.

In 1983 Chuck said, "You've got to come back to St. Louis and run the tool group from here." He had made another major acquisition, Appleton Electric, which made explosive proof conduit boxes. He wanted to add that to my portfolio and have George Sherman take over SKIL. Appleton Electric began reporting to me while I still lived in Chicago. Chuck allowed me to stay in Chicago after George took over SKIL because of my family. However, I knew we had to move because I was spending way too much time traveling and staying in St. Louis hotels. So we moved back to St. Louis in July 1983.

I was becoming increasingly involved in issues and decisions related to the central corporate operation and less involved in the management of SKIL. My new position in St. Louis was executive vice president, with the tool group reporting to me. It was well over $1 billion operation, perhaps even closer to $2 billion. The move was a typical path for someone with my background, and I was somewhat familiar with corporate because I had been in St. Louis so often. In fact, up to five or six months before I moved, I was attending the same meetings that the other segment leaders attended. The only difference was I came in from Chicago. So when the meeting ended on Saturday morning I just caught a plane and went back to Chicago.

Two significant events occurred after my return to St. Louis. Emerson made a major acquisition of a company, SKB Industrial Group, owned by SmithKline Beckman. It was actually four companies primarily involved in electronic components. This moved me into an entirely new area. Moving from the rather mundane products of Browning Manufacturing with v-belts sheaves and sprockets to a portable electric tool is one step. But it is a major step to then go into electronics, which is driven by a higher level of quality, massive quantities, and demanding customers like IBM.

Nevertheless, Emerson, "in its infinite wisdom," pulled me out of the tool business and put me in charge of the four electronic units. The main reason they put me in charge was not because of my knowledge of the business but because we had to move them and I had operational experience in relocating plants. These units were located at the SmithKline Beckman campus in Fullerton, California. They wanted the space to expand their pharmaceutical operations and wanted us out of the way within a year.

One year is a quick turnaround for a complex production operation to be relocated. To compound matters, Bill Rutledge, Emerson's chief operating officer and a great man who came from GE, developed a weak heart muscle. His doctor told him, "You just can't stay under this kind of pressure and get better. You must take six months off so your heart can strengthen." When he took the time off, Chuck now had me running half the company and another person, Al Suter, running the other half, and we were both on the Emerson Board because of our new responsibilities. Rutledge was already serving on the board, kept attending the board meetings despite doctor's orders for a few months but he subsequently retired. The participation during the board meetings gave me some insight into the role of the COO without being the chief operating officer. I felt this experience is how I earned my wings and eventually was named the chief operating officer. I had direct responsibility for my units and then took over half the company and moved to a reporting relationship to the CEO. We also experienced a terrible economic downturn during this time. I think that surviving the downturn was probably one of the key issues in positioning me for a move further up the corporate ladder.

Due to the recession, corporate sponsors began pulling out of NASCAR, golf tournaments, and other sporting events. Always somewhat counterintuitive, Chuck Knight decided it was the best time for Emerson to begin sponsoring IndyCar races. In addition,

Chuck declared, "We're going to fund IndyCar sponsorship out of next year's budget." I reminded Chuck we were having a hard time making any budgets at all. Undeterred, Chuck shot back, "Well, the recession won't last forever." Sure enough, as Chuck predicted and before we had to put our first dollar in IndyCar, our profits began to return to pre-recession levels. I had no experience with corporate sponsorships for sports ventures, but within a couple of years the IndyCar sponsorship reported to me. My son and I had attended an IndyCar race in Milwaukee when we lived in Chicago and I had been to the Indianapolis 500 a couple of times. It would never have entered my mind to put money into IndyCar. But it was successful as it gave us a platform to meet and entertain many customers and new prospects.

Once I had a seat on the Emerson Board, I gained access to even more information and I had the opportunity to get to know the other board members. The board had sixteen members which, in my opinion, was too many. The board also included five Emerson employees. It was somewhat unusual to have that large of a percentage of board members comprised of employees. I had a seat at the table and a chair with my name engraved on a small gold plate. But my name was attached by screws so I always knew it could come off as easily as it had gone on.

As an employee on the board, I knew I should not just jump right into the debates among the members because I was still working for the board. If I saw something not quite right in another segment of the company, I would not speak up in the board meeting. I waited until we moved into our own little closed meeting to discuss it. Being on the board was an honor and brought with it a certain amount of prestige. I probably did not add any more substance to the board than presenting to them regarding my individual area and then leaving the room. Being on the board as an employee was a plus for me but not so much for the board. Still, overall, it was good for the company because of the breadth of knowledge I gained and the sense of ownership one feels in the company.

Additionally, even as powerful as Chuck was within the company, he could not have made me president of Emerson if the board had not had some exposure to me alongside the other candidates. Following Rutledge's retirement, Chuck had to start thinking about what to do with the title of president and ultimately decided not to fill the position but to assume the title himself. I am sure that during organizational discussions Chuck talked to the board about their candidates. One of Chuck's greatest attributes was his ability to put the right people in the right positions around him. He worked at that. For example, he would go to a meeting somewhere and notice someone who seemed very talented. Chuck would recruit that person to Emerson even if we had no position available for them at the time. We would have to scurry around and try to separate responsibilities out of a division or two for the new person to do until something else opened up.

Most of my contributions to Emerson were strictly operational. I benefited from having a boss who drove home the importance of strategic planning and acquisitions. At that time Emerson would look at over six hundred leads a year as possible acquisitions. We had an entire department responsible for reviewing the companies under consideration and culling the list down to maybe fifty that Emerson would look at for roughly a thirty-minute review. Then the list would be cut down from fifty to around ten. Those ten were then sent to operations to explore synergies with existing Emerson divisions. Maybe one or two of the companies would ultimately be considered as having attributes that meshed with Emerson's strategic plans or brought something to Emerson that we were not already making. Primarily we were looking at the acquisition to see if we could combine or shoulder it up against one of our thirty divisions. At that point, I might or might not be briefly involved in the process for any particular acquisition. Regardless, on any given day someone might come into my office, hand me a very large binder, and announce, "Here is a new company for you. We're closing on the purchase Friday at 2:30."

My ability to bring new acquisitions into Emerson was probably my biggest accomplishment between 1983 and 1989. In this role I had to motivate as well as chew out division presidents, and yet maintain a good working relationship, whether they were newly acquired companies or not. To be successful in this role, I had to get over feeling that they thought I did not know about or understand their business. Division presidents would stonewall me in a heartbeat just because I represented corporate. I simply dealt with that and did not let it worry me. Any successful corporate leader must learn to operate that way.

I kept track of the companies in my area by establishing a system they knew well and felt comfortable putting information into or, in some cases, trying to get around. When doing an onsite visit I really tried to focus on the business at hand and I rarely took phone calls. Of course, that was easier to do then because we did not have cell phones. I did not look away when someone talked to me and I gave them my full attention. I tried to be a member of their staff that day and it worked. During my onsite visits I gained a better understanding of the operation's potential and what they needed to do to reach their goals. I also established good rapport with the leadership at the sites.

I was able to share many suggestions for improvement to the companies because Chuck provided me with good ideas. He would not let me fail and was always there when I needed him. I was well equipped with experience and management skills, but it always came down to relationships up and down the corporate ladder. Of course, there were some bumps along the road because I did not get along with the leadership in every company. In those instances, I consulted with the person between me and the person with whom I was having a problem. I would say, "You know, this just isn't clicking. It may be me or it may be that we have a problem. Regardless, it is one of the two and you've got to sort this thing out before it ends badly."

I enjoyed this time at Emerson immensely. It was a serious time for Emerson because we were attempting to hold onto a record of earnings improvement quarter by quarter that we did not want to lose. Our reputation for success was a great motivator for me and the company as a whole. If I had a problem in one area, I knew I had to find the solution in another area to make up for it, because that was just the way it worked.

Chuck was very demanding. I remember many difficult meetings with him, and quite often those meetings were at his home on Sunday mornings. Sometimes Chuck could be very difficult to help. In one instance, we were all schooling Chuck as he prepared for the annual meeting of stockholders. Chuck resented those sessions because he did not like for us to tell him he was doing anything incorrectly. So we always tried to deliver any criticism very gently. During Chuck's presentation at one annual stockholders' meeting, a gentleman got up who looked like he could have been a college professor. He was wearing a tweed jacket with leather patches on the elbows. He asked, "Mr. Chairman, I'd like to know how many plants you have north of I-30 in Iowa." Chuck looked down at us in the front row and barked, "Why didn't you smart guys think of that question?" Turns out the questioner lived in northern Iowa and wanted to know if he could get something to help their economy. But, as time has passed, I tend to remember only the fun parts about working with Chuck at Emerson.

At this point in 1988–1989, I had made more money than I ever thought possible and I had risen to the top ranks of a great corporation. But I do not think one has it made until your reputation goes beyond where you are. For example, when I was at Emerson it never entered my mind that I was particularly successful or particularly secure. Certainly, I knew I had made some significant accomplishments and I was going to get three strikes before I was out. But the idea of slackening my pace never entered my mind. I continued to be motivated because I did not want to fail, even though I had already succeeded by most any measure.

Perhaps because I am an engineer, I have always been very conscious of time. I thought I should work until I was sixty-five and no one ever told me any different. Whatever success I have had was built one day at a time and perhaps by not making too many really bad decisions. Actually, a lot of the decisions I made ended up being more positive than I thought they would. In every position I held, I always kept an eye out for the next step for me to move up the line at Emerson Electric or elsewhere. Because of Emerson's excellent reputation as a well-managed corporation, I would receive feelers from headhunters representing corporations whose identity I did not even know.

Frederick W. Wackerle, a Chicago-based executive recruiter, played an important role in my move to Textron as COO. He encouraged me to consider the position even when I was not sure I should be contemplating a move. He phoned me in the spring of 1989 and, after introducing himself, told me he had taken on an assignment for a company that wanted to know if I would be willing to make a career move. When I asked him who he was representing, he told me he was not at liberty to identify the corporation but they were looking at me as well as two internal candidates.

As soon as he said that, I stopped him in mid-sentence and said, "I'm very satisfied with my position at Emerson and I have an excellent future right here. I have absolutely no interest in getting into a situation in which I am not the frontrunner for a position." He called me back later and said both internal candidates had dropped out of consideration and the corporation was definitely going to hire someone from the outside. He then told me he represented a multi-industry corporation based on the East Coast. I finally said, "Well, I do think I have management talents to bring to a multi-industry corporation where I would be working with a number of units. I'll come and talk to you."

At that point I had no idea which corporation he represented. Since he mentioned the East Coast, I figured it was a corporation headquartered in New York or New Jersey. I had never traveled to Rhode Island and was unaware that it was home to a major corporation.

So in August 1989, I met Fred Wackerle at the Bob O'Link Country Club near Lake Forest, where we used to live. We discussed the position in general terms and I reviewed with him what I considered to be my accomplishments. I also explained to him as candidly as possible how I saw my future if I stayed at Emerson. I knew I would likely never be their chief executive officer, even if I remained at Emerson for the rest of my career.

Chuck was a year younger than me and frankly, I think he was better than me. But Chuck told me many times, "Before I retire I want you to be CEO." The problem as I saw it was that even if I had been named CEO, Chuck would have continued as chairman and with that arrangement I could never have functioned as a true CEO. I never got too excited about Chuck's "plan" for my future.

I had told Wackerle that I could not consider any change without talking with Gay. He said they would not identify the corporation until I had talked with her. After consulting with Gay, we decided to see how it all played out. Subsequently, I met the corporation's CEO in New York at the Bull and Bear Restaurant in the Waldorf Astoria Hotel. I can still see the two-person table located by the window. Beverly Dolan introduced himself and identified his corporation as Textron. He had been CEO of Textron since 1979. I still did not know what the corporation did because as it was a holding company, you could only see the financials of thirty-one different brands. Once he mentioned Bell Helicopter, Homelite Chainsaw, and Greenlee Tools as components of Textron, I could then relate. As a holding corporation, they owned the companies and all of the financials flowed in and they put them all together.

Soon after, Jim Martin, a senior director, Beverly Dolan, and their spouses came to St. Louis to talk with Gay and me. We met them in a suite at a downtown hotel. During this recruitment process I found myself flying one day on an Emerson plane and the next day flying on a Textron plane. In one instance I flew into St. Louis on an Emerson plane, had someone drive me to another corporate hangar, and boarded a Textron plane to fly somewhere else. I still had not talked with anyone at Emerson.

Textron invited Gay and me to Providence, where we had dinner on a Friday evening with Bill Wayland, head of Textron's human resources department. The next day they took us on a helicopter tour of Rhode Island which, since it's a small state, did not take very long. At noon we had lunch with Beverly Dolan and his wife at a country club and that evening some other people joined us. We left the next day, still not knowing where we stood.

In November 1989, as I was preparing to leave for Japan, I received a call from Bill Wayland telling me Textron wanted me as their president and chief operating officer. I said, "Look, I must make this trip to Japan because all of the plans have been finalized for the people over there." Bill Wayland was a very professional human resources manager who had previously worked for Chrysler and had now been at Textron for several years. He responded, "You know how these things are. We're ready to make a decision." That likely meant they had at least one or two other people waiting in the wings. I told Bill, "All right, here's what I will do. I'll fly up to Chicago on Saturday afternoon since I'm flying out of Chicago to go to Japan."

At that point, we had not discussed salary or other compensation issues, but he said he planned to bring all of the terms of the offer to me. I had already given Textron my salary requirements to make the move and they gave me every reason to believe they were not turned off by those numbers. So we met, discussed the terms, and I signed the contract. They assured me they would not announce my hiring until I returned from Japan because I still had not talked with Chuck or anyone from Emerson. I wanted to tell Chuck as soon as I got home, but it was Thanksgiving week and he was out of town.

The following Monday I convened Emerson's President's Council meeting. All divisions came to the council meeting to report their plans for the foreseeable future. With the Textron issue hanging over my head, I felt like I was in the wrong place. But fortunately Chuck was back in town and we had one of our regularly scheduled dinners on Monday night. We met at the St. Louis Club and began reviewing the agenda items we had each prepared.

Chuck had only gotten through the third item on his list when I thought, "I can't take this." So I interrupted him and said, "Chuck, I've been offered a position at Textron which I have accepted." He did not see it coming and looked like I had punched him in the stomach. Recovering somewhat, he asked, "What is the position?" I told him, "I'm going in as their president and COO." He reminded me, "But you already have that title with us." I replied, "Yes, but they told me their CEO is going to retire in twelve months." He shot back angrily, "You believe all that stuff?" I said I knew I was taking a bit of a chance but was confident it would all work out as planned. Chuck said, "I guess we have nothing to talk about. You go on and—" I interrupted him to quickly add, "I can stay through the end of the year." He said, "Well, we'll see about that." We ate our salads, making awkward conversation, and we both left before our main courses arrived.

I went into the office the next day and we completed the President's Council work on the fourth day of meetings. On the last day Chuck came into the conference room after the meeting adjourned and looked at the meeting notes on flip chart pages hanging on the walls that showed how we were doing. Then he said, "I'd like to see you when you're finished down here." A few minutes later I went into Chuck's office, where he had a round table in the middle with stacks of papers on it. Without any small talk and barely looking up, he said, "I want your credit cards, I want the keys to your car, and I want you to clean out your office tonight." Somewhat surprised by his abrupt instructions, I did what he asked and called Gay to come and get me since I no longer had a car.

After three days thinking about my departure, Chuck was steaming. Emerson had threatened Textron that they would go ahead and announce I was gone and name my replacement. Textron had to scramble to get a press release out on my appointment. I had to scurry around to reach Ray Caine, Textron's vice president of Corporate Communications. Ray later became one of my eight or ten closest friends from my Textron days. I had not met Ray before but I reached him by phone and said, "We need to drum up an announcement or you're going to look like you are getting damaged goods." So he contacted Bill Anderson at Fleishman-Hillard, who handled all of Emerson's external communications. I had already called Bill and of course he already knew about my resignation and was preparing a press release. So cooler heads prevailed and the release went out that evening, to be announced the next morning.

The Emerson President's Council held their end-of-meeting dinner that same evening. One of the board members arrived late, looked around, and asked, "Where's Jim?" Someone pointed to a copy of the press release. I began getting phone calls at home that evening as people learned I was leaving Emerson. It turned into one of the longest nights of my life.

The next morning I realized that, for the first time in a very long time, I was unemployed. I called Textron and explained that I did not know what I would do for the next month. They seemed to understand my need to be doing something and they told me just to come to work. Several Textron officials were on their way to Nashville for a meeting, so the following morning, December 1, they flew into St. Louis, picked me up, and I went to the meeting in Nashville. I was back, no longer unemployed.

After twenty-eight years with Emerson Electric, this is how my career with them ended. I knew I had really hurt Chuck and he thought it was a blow to the company when I did not wait it out to become CEO of Emerson. I was one of the first senior people ever to leave Emerson. Later, when it was announced that I had been named CEO of Textron, Chuck was the first person to call and congratulate me. Time had lessened his disappointment and we were able to kid around and continue our friendship. It actually reflected well on Emerson management that I, and eventually others, left Emerson to run major companies and corporations.

Looking back, deciding to leave Emerson at the age of fifty-five was probably riskier than I wanted to believe at the time. A lot of people make career decisions in their fifties that turn out to be terrible mistakes. One problem is that one is getting close to a time where you are too old to make a new start in another position, even though you might not be too old for the position you already have. In my case, I had mentally taken one step at a time in my career and the opportunity to run a multi-industry corporation was just too tantalizing to pass up, regardless of the risks. I had been approached for other positions that were all focused on a certain industry. In those cases, I knew I would be going in with a bunch of people who had been there all their lives and it would have been hard to bring anything fresh to the position. Prior to Textron, I had developed a proven process for managing and had a reputation for hard work. I just felt that it was the right move at the right time and I went for it.

Before I went to Providence, fourteen members of the Textron board had interviewed me at the 21 Club in New York. Everyone shook hands before we sat down but, as is true of most boards, just three members of this one dominated the conversation. I quickly understood the board was very dependent on those three people and the CEO. It was an unusual interview in that only three people said a word, and I have never had another one like it before or since. But the board made me feel welcome and the interview went well. Afterwards, I learned there were some board members concerned about bringing a southerner with an obvious accent into a heavily Catholic, northeastern-educated environment. Since I was coming from Emerson, an international corporation with an excellent reputation, it never occurred to me that my background might be of concern.

I could not believe the generous terms of my contract with Textron. I had never had a contract like it. The contract provided even greater financial security than we had experienced up to that point. If I failed at Textron, we would have been fine financially, but it would have been a tremendous disappointment and a blow to my reputation because of the respect I had worked hard to earn over the previous decades.

During my first few weeks in Providence in 1989 it was brutally cold. I stayed in the Omni Hotel, then the only hotel in downtown Providence. It was so cold I had to pile my overcoat on top of the blankets on my bed to stay warm. I was even required to take a drug test, which was the first indication that I was not totally in command. The government had just enacted a policy that required defense contractor employees working on either defense or aerospace items be subject to random drug testing. Even though the government was requiring the drug tests, we were having a little trouble convincing our unions to agree to them. Bell Helicopter, particularly, had a large union and our human resources people told me that if I would submit to a drug test, it would help sell the notion to the unions. So even before we moved, Gay and I drove up to Pawtucket, Rhode Island. We took one look at the old building we were about to enter for the test when Gay turned to me and said, "A person could catch something in there!" Nevertheless, I took the drug test and two or three days later the report came back. Fortunately, I passed.

As usual, Gay handled the heavy lifting to find us a new home. She found a house in Barrington, thirteen miles outside of Providence, and to this day it remains my favorite house. Our property was located on a Narragansett Bay inlet, affording us a good view of the water from our house. The commute was much easier than most of my previous commutes and when I returned home each day, I felt good about where we lived. Contrary to anywhere else we had lived, our social life was mostly limited to company-related events, primarily because our children were grown and gone. Gay and I agreed we would focus our time and energies in Rhode Island on the company and people associated with Textron. We rented a home in Florida and Gay would stay there for a month or two every winter. I tried to join her in Florida whenever possible, but the rest of the time we were in Providence.

I had time to familiarize myself with the company without pressure because there had been no COO prior to me. Textron was founded by Royal Little, who lived in Narragansett, Rhode Island. He was an investor who began his career when he privately bought a couple of companies. One company was a foundry and the other was a textile business. This is where the name Textron came from. Little just kept buying companies and eventually went public with their stock.

A 1960s Harvard study named Textron as the business world's first conglomerate, which is a company comprised of a variety of different types of businesses. Little did not want any two divisions to be alike so that an economic downturn in any one part of the company would not be devastating to the entire company. Over time Textron was comprised of everything from eyeglass lenses to staplers to chainsaws to Bell Helicopters. But Little's base of operations for the company remained in Providence because it was the center of the state where he lived.

Textron had owned Bostich Staplers, located in Westerly, Rhode Island, but the company had been sold before I came. We still owned Speidel Watch Band but later sold it. We also owned a commercial finance company. So we still had quite a few employees in the state when I arrived. But at that time the company basically was driven by defense. And that may have been another questionable decision on my part. About 40 percent of the company was defense—and I went there in 1989, the year the Berlin Wall came down. So the Cold War was suddenly over. However, this turned out to be a plus because it drove Textron to make changes to the company. We operated some good defense businesses like Bell Helicopter but we had some that were not very high in share. I felt it was time for Textron to begin buying more industrial companies while selling off the rest of the consumer businesses. Over the next ten years we would do a lot of buying and selling.

Skyline of Maysville, Kentucky, 2007. (Courtesy of Nealparr at the English
Wikipedia [CC BY-SA 3.0 (http://creativecommons.org/licenses/by-sa/3.0/)]

Kenneth T. and Pauline Strode Hardymon

Jim Hardymon (second from left second row) at the completion of basic training at Ft. Knox, Kentucky, December, 1958. He reported to Ft. Dix, New Jersey the following month.

The Sigma Alpha Epsilon House, University of Kentucky, located at 230 South Limestone during Hardymon's time at UK. (Courtesy of University of Kentucky Libraries)

Jim and Gay Hardymon married June 25, 1960. They are seen here standing in front of the James F. Harydmon Building on the UK campus. Dedicated in September 2000, the Hardymon Building is home to the Alliance for Networking Excellence, the Laboratory for Advanced Networking, other laboratories and offices of Computer Science, and offices of Information Technology. (Courtesy of Univerity of Kentucky Office of Public Relations)

Jim Hardymon (bottom row, third from the right) pictured with Browning Manufacturing sales team in 1964 at the Maysville, Kentucky railroad depot.

Larry Browning was serving as executive vice-president and chief operating officer of Browning Manufacturing in Maysville in 1969 when he
negotiated the merger of Browning into Emerson Electric. He later became
Vice-Chairman of Emerson Electric. (Photo courtesy of Webster University
and the Browning family)

Emerson Electric leadership team. Charles F. "Chuck" Knight seated and Hardymon standing to his right.

President George H.W. Bush and Jim Hardymon.

Jim Hardymon and President Bill Clinton at the presidential inauguration

The stone entrances to the University of Kentucky were funded during President Charles T. Wethington's administration by a gift from Jim and Gay Hardymon. (Courtesy of University of Kentucky Office of Public Relations)

Jim Hardymon speaking at the dedication of the Donovan and Johnson residence halls, August 12, 2013. Seated to his left is UK President Eli Capilouto. Hardymon played a pivotal role in the development of UK's public/private partnership for the construction of new residence halls. (Courtesy of University of Kentucky Office of Public Relations)

Students utilizing the new James F. and Gay Hardymon Student Success Center located in the UK College of Engineering. This Center, dedicated in 2017, was made possible by a 3.5 million dollar gift from Jim and Gay Hardymon as well as additional funding toward an endowment for the college's undergraduate research and education abroad programs. (Courtesy of University of Kentucky College of Engineering)

(Left to right) Dr. Mary Lynne Capilouto, Gay Hardymon, Jim Hardymon, and UK President Eli Capilouto. (Courtesy of University of Kentucky College of Engineering)

Jim Hardymon honored as one of four outstanding corporate directors in 2004 by the Outstanding Directors Exchange (ODX) and Columbia Business School's Executive Education division. At the time Hardymon was serving as a director for Air Products and Chemicals, Inc., American Standard Companies, Inc., Circuit City Stores, Inc. and Lexmark International, Inc. (Used with permission of © Kenneth Hayden, Louisville, Kentucky)

The Hardymon family, December, 2016. Seated L-R: Emma Hardymon, Jim Hardymon, Gay Hardymon, Grace Hardymon. Standing L-R: Frank Sovich, Jennifer Sovich, Christopher Sovich, Caroline Sovich Branham, Josh Branham, Lisa Hardymon, and Frank Hardymon.

I studied my new company for a few weeks, and the first few days around the office were tough. During the most difficult parts I wondered if I had made the right decision. Both the environment and the people were very different from what I had experienced at Emerson. Initially I had not given much thought to those differences because the CEO before me came from Augusta, Georgia, and he returned to the South after leaving Textron. The human resources person, Bill Wayland, had lived in England and New York a good while so he was not your typical New Englander either. Like a lot of people, I lumped Boston and Providence together, and many of the Textron leadership held Harvard degrees.

Textron headquarters were in downtown Providence, known as "the biggest city in the smallest state in the US." My biggest frustration was my inability to gain access to my office on weekends. I was literally locked out; if I wanted to enter the building I had to ring a bell. I had never experienced anything like that before. Our building had twenty-three floors and one security guard on weekends. So the security guard could be walking around anywhere in the building when I needed to get in. I had to stand and wait at the door until he came and unlocked it. Also, the parking garage was not open, requiring me to park on the street. And this was even before more intense security measures kicked in after 9/11.

I worked closely with Herb Henkel holding planning sessions that were basically strategic reviews. We did not examine each quarter but took a longer view of operations. Herb and I went out to Rockford, Illinois, to visit our operation there. I took along a binder full of company information that I had studied and I asked our people in Rockford a lot of questions. On the way to the airport late that afternoon following the all-day visit, Herb looked over at me, smiled broadly, and remarked, "Jim, you should know that no one before you ever visited a site longer than two hours, and they never asked questions."

After a few months with Textron I could sense that Dolan

was ready to relinquish the CEO position. I was confident that I would get the job when he left or, at least, that it was mine to lose. At the time of my move to Textron the company gave me a carefully written letter from Textron stating, essentially, that the CEO decision would be made within a specific timeframe but it did not guarantee that I would become the CEO. Fortunately, it all worked out: I was named CEO in late 1991.

Large companies are organized like pyramids and the walls get pretty narrow for a CEO by the time they get to the top. Moreover, the larger the company, the narrower those walls feel. I made a large number of personnel changes, but over time, I only had five people reporting directly to me and we met weekly.

My position as CEO of Textron required a more public role than my previous positions with Emerson in either St. Louis or Chicago. Our marketing people made many suggestions to me about public relations strategies. I went on the board of United Way because Textron had always been very involved with that organization. I was familiar with United Way from my time at SKIL. I also went on the board of Fleet Bank, the largest bank in Providence, whose main offices were across the street from Textron. I found serving on the bank board to be very beneficial.

I also had to adjust to local politics, which were nothing like any I had seen before. Buddy Cianci first became mayor of Providence in 1974. He resigned after a felony conviction for attacking a man he thought was having an affair with his estranged wife. Cianci hosted a popular radio talk show when we first arrived, but by 1990 he had won a three-way race for mayor of Providence by only 709 votes. Naturally, I would often find myself at events in the city with Mayor Cianci. I was always somewhat anxious when he spoke in public because I never knew what he might say about Textron.

Many wondered why Textron remained in Providence when we could have moved anywhere and other cities could offer so much more. But after purchasing the building we had been leasing, Mayor Cianci seemed to settle down and his stories became a little more complimentary of Textron. Nevertheless, Cianci's second term as mayor also ended with a felony conviction—and this time he went to prison.

In retrospect, I moved to Textron at a good time.

Chapter Four

Transforming an International Conglomerate

In the business world, the easiest way
to measure success is financial.
For me, that is the scorecard.

We did not rush into a divestiture and acquisition process during my first couple of years at Textron, but I began to seriously explore what changes could be made that would positively impact the company. When I arrived, Textron, an $8 billion conglomerate that would eventually become a $14 billion conglomerate, had twenty-five different units that submitted their financials individually. Each unit was audited and their financials were approved centrally. But because each unit submitted their financial information differently, it was difficult to consolidate the data in a meaningful way that allowed us to forecast Textron's future earnings. We could forecast for each division but not for the entire company. We put in place strategies that required more uniformity in financial reporting from each unit. We also transferred personnel between units much more than had been done in the past. Quite simply, we needed to get our financial house in order before moving on to larger initiatives.

Fortunately, a few months before I arrived the board and the previous CEO decided to take some major write-offs in the third calendar quarter of 1989. This decision put the company in a good position to begin to move forward. Textron had not paid a dividend for five years and had a high debt to capital ratio, in the range of 30–40 percent. So we had to make a few smaller adjustments to get the company creating cash and making some profits to overcome these write-offs, which created a loss in the quarter that they occurred.

We increased dramatically the number of mergers and acquisitions. By analyzing the current structure of Textron, we found some obvious pieces that were going to be a problem, such as Homelite, the chainsaw business. Consumer chainsaw sales had declined since the end of the 1970s energy crisis. Additionally, after the Cold War ended people thought there would be peace forever with plenty of oil to go around. Our debt to equity ratio was somewhere in the area of 30–40 percent and we needed to bring it down in the 20 percent range. Being able to sell off pieces of the company allowed us to do that.

It became apparent very quickly that defense was an area that could hurt us down the road. Defense brought in $1.2 billion in annual revenue at that time. Textron's total revenue was about $8 billion so we knew we were going to get hurt if we did not find something to replace it. I immediately began talking with the banks.

Morgan Stanley, our advisor at the time, suggested that we create an investor relations department. Textron's lack of an investor relations department caused Textron stock to fluctuate more than normal. So we moved very quickly on the recommendation. Gay and I had met Ed Arditte when we had lunch with the CEO at the Rhode Island Country Club. He was on his way out to play golf and he just struck me as someone I would like to work more closely with at some point. So I moved him out of the treasury department and put him in as head of Textron's investor relations department.

It was about this time that a board member admitted, "It's probably time we look at things a little differently." I could tell that, at least on the part of some of the board members, change was not only wanted but expected. That attitude among the board members gave me a lot of flexibility. That meant I did not have to wait for something negative to occur to make substantial changes like selling parts of the company or acquiring other companies.

Rapid changes in the defense industry as a result of the end of the Cold War provided plenty of incentive for us to make changes. We immediately began evaluating our businesses by assessing their strengths for the long haul versus businesses that would likely continue to get weaker due to changes in the business climate. Perhaps the Textron board did not entirely anticipate the number of changes I subsequently made. Given the circumstances, Textron would likely have made major changes even if I had not joined the firm. But I was the CEO and I did what I thought needed to be done in the best interest of the company.

When you go through the process of buying companies, you buy them for the price that you and the seller negotiate. Then you also have something known as book value. Book value is established by means of various financial procedures. If the purchase price for a company is higher than the book value, the difference is referred to as "goodwill." Goodwill is a burden because it must be written off over a certain number of years. If you acquire too many pieces of a business that have a higher payment price than the book value, and you are therefore carrying a high goodwill, you have a hard time making enough money to overcome that particular write-off every quarter.

So Textron wrote down a number of their businesses to a more realistic value and took a one-time hit to get the goodwill down. That put those businesses in a much better position to sell if we chose to. If we thought we could do better with them by increasing the earnings, we could overcome the goodwill and in turn increase the earnings.

The reason that we as a team decided to shed some of our defense businesses was because they were not particularly strong. For example, we made the turbine engine for the Adams sixty-ton tank. When the Berlin Wall came down, the need for tanks running up and down the autobahns in Germany for defense purposes mostly went away. Suddenly, we started seeing small military flare-ups around the world in places that had deserts or swamps and a sixty-ton tank was not needed, and therefore the engines for the tanks were not needed.

We chose to not sell Bell Helicopter because we believed that the need for helicopters would remain steady or even increase. We knew it was a good business, and additionally, Bell had research projects under way for which it would have been difficult to determine a value. At that time they were not creating any value but we thought they would in the future, which made Bell Helicopter a very hard company to sell. So Textron stayed in the defense business to that extent.

The defense businesses started consolidating and realized they needed to change significantly in order to survive. A successful company could no longer make just one type of military product because as conflicts changed, the needs of the military changed. Also, each time leadership within the Defense Department changed, the types of products they wanted often changed as well. Moreover, requests for product fluctuated among the different branches of the armed forces.

In the midst of repositioning our existing companies, Textron bought Avco Consumer Financial Services. Because Avco was as large as Textron, the purchase was like biting off something too big to swallow. But the way to purchase a company of similar size or larger is to borrow money. The borrowing is justified by having a business plan that shows how profits will be derived from the new addition. The most logical approach to acquiring a large business is to integrate it with other pieces within the company. There were many pieces to Textron and we determined that the best leveraging possibility with the Avco acquisition was with defense and ultimately with finance. But at the same time we bought Avco, the United States entered one of the few periods since World War II where defense spending was flat or increasing only slightly.

The opportunity to purchase Avco came from outside Textron and was not created by me and my management team. Perhaps anyone sitting in the CEO chair at Textron could have seen the same opportunity and moved on it. The only question might have been whether or not they would have seen the consolidation going on in the defense business. Lockheed Martin and a few other major defense contractors decided they were going to acquire additional defense businesses and thus become a bigger portion of the remaining defense pie. The big question that arose for Textron was whether we should sell off even more of our defense-related businesses and become more like General Dynamics.

My plan to redirect Textron did involve products. I was not driven by finance businesses and I felt we should get out of that business sector. At that time, we owned Paul Revere Disability Income Insurance and Avco Consumer Loans, both large companies. My management team and I began the process of selling the insurance company. But Wall Street wanted us to break off the finance group from the manufacturing group and have two separate companies with two separate stocks. The manufacturing group was not large enough to stand alone so we had to feed it acquisitions in order to enlarge it. Finally, we sold both finance companies.

During 1990–1991 we experienced a slight downturn in the economy. It was not good for President George H. W. Bush because he lost his reelection bid. But in some ways the downturn helped us because of the restructuring we had under way and we were coming off a relatively moderate, to say the least, track record. So it was easy for us to have a gradual improvement, although we were not hitting any home runs.

The perception of a company's success has a lot to do with size and the return on equity, ROE. If that return could be pushed up to 15 or 16 percent, that would place you in one level. If Textron could match Emerson at about 20 percent, that would be another level. GE at 23 percent was the highest level. A big stockholder trying to put together a diversified portfolio will have some of these types of companies in there. We were trying to get to the level of GE, which had a long run as one of the world's leading companies but is not doing as well now. But in those days, it was GE and maybe one or two others that sat at the top. We constantly tried to get into that level where stock moves by transactions. Stocks stay at the same price forever if somebody does not buy it or sell it.

I am very competitive and I wanted to succeed at Textron. Moreover, the company offered me a package that in addition to salary brought me company stock. As the company did better, I did better. In the business world, the easiest way to measure success is financial. For me, that is the scorecard. There are many other ways to be successful other than just being able to accumulate financial well-being. But it was very common in the corporate world then, when the stock market was generally going up, to give an executive stock options based on prices at that time, with the incentive being that if you stay, you are going to make quite a bit more money. So, instead of giving a corporate leader a salary that offers him or her an annual pay increase of a certain amount, a company can choose to offer less in salary and more in stock options.

Textron experienced three pretty good years in 1990, 1991, and 1992, and began moving up. To this day, I still do not know how it happened but word got out about me being on a list for other CEO jobs. Nobody ever called or interviewed me. I was fifty-eight years old and could probably have done one more move. So Textron came up with a plan to give me at that point all of the stock options I would have gotten between then and when I turned sixty-five, meaning they front-loaded my stock options. They gave me five hundred thousand shares that turned into a million when we later split the stock. If I stayed with the company until retirement, they offered to give me, in cash, the difference between the value of Textron stock in 1992 and 1999.

In 1992 Textron stock was at $24 a share and by 1999 it reached $74 a share—and I owned 1 million shares. My arrangement with Textron was somewhat unusual. I do not believe the board, in their wildest dreams, ever thought it would be that much money. If I had waited and retired in 2001, it would have been much less.

The funny thing is that I had not been contacted about other positions. And the only other position I would even have considered would have been leading a diversified company. That was my expertise and what I enjoyed. I flew 250,000 air miles a year as our companies were located around the globe. I probably visited an average of three businesses a week. I went from helicopters to chainsaws to golf carts to turf care equipment to tools to airplanes. Each had their different product liability and purchasing issues. I was comfortable and I seemed to have a knack for making abrupt changes such as going from turbine engines to golf carts in forty-eight hours. I recognized that was a talent that I brought to the position and so that is where I stayed. I would not have gone anywhere else.

When I arrived at the company, much of Textron focused on military business. I had very little experience with military manufacturing at Emerson. So this emphasis at Textron was somewhat different for me. There were two military-focused divisions that actually comprised 25 percent of Textron: Bell Helicopter and turban engines made by the Textron Aerospace Division. There were four new things that I had not dealt with: automotive, defense, going to the stock market and talking to the individuals, and dealing with Washington. One might think that defense and Washington are the same thing, but it is not the case.

Of course, you cannot have military business without lobbying and a Washington connection. I had not been to Washington since my honeymoon. There were people at Emerson who dealt with Washington, but I was never invited to participate. Textron maintained a Washington office that worked well. We had employees who basically worked as lobbyists. But we also utilized outside lobbyists. Our people knew all the right people, such as the big players on defense appropriations. If I went to see the secretary of defense, who at the time was Dick Cheney, they went with me. My meetings with Cheney were not very pleasant.

In conjunction with Boeing, we were building an experimental helicopter called the V22 or Osprey. It took off like a helicopter and then the engines rotated to become a fixed-wing aircraft. It has been used extensively in Iraq and Afghanistan. The Osprey was a multi-use military item. Cheney wanted to kill the Osprey but keep the Boeing CH46, which could carry only troops. The Osprey could stay in the air from San Francisco to Hawaii, which was then the longest over-water run in the world. It could hover with ten thousand pounds in a sling hanging underneath. It could also carry twenty-five troops and, of course, it could fly at a faster speed than a helicopter. But its success was touch and go.

The first Osprey accident happened when the test pilot and the co-pilot were trying to hover and it slammed back to the ground. One of the pilots broke his ankle but nobody was seriously injured. Ironically, the second accident happened while an Osprey was en route to Washington to put the aircraft on display for Congress. That crash killed several people, making the prospects for the Osprey even more difficult. Moreover, the production costs kept going up.

Cheney continued his opposition to the Osprey while Representative John Murtha from Pennsylvania and Governor Ann Richards of Texas pushed to keep production going. Our Washington office also continued working hard to maintain support for the project. But every meeting I had with Cheney centered on the Osprey, and I found him a very hard man to talk to because I did not think he was listening. Perhaps he just did not want to hear anymore about the Osprey. But we found others to support it.

It was important for Textron and for me to become more involved in our Washington and Wall Street efforts. I think the Textron Board understood my strengths and weaknesses. They understood my strength was operations and that I would go out in those factories and find some efficiency improvement just by walking through the plants. But they were concerned I might never leave the factories, so we actually came up with the number of days I was to spend on Wall Street and the number of times I would go to Washington.

During my visits to Wall Street, I talked either with investors or those who were advising investors. We referred to it as going to visit the analyst because they were analyzing these companies. Sometimes we had small meetings in which there were normally two of us and two or three of them, with one of them being the leader. Other times we had seminars, like when Goldman Sachs would put on a three-day meeting these analysts could attend and hear maybe seventeen companies present individually. For example, we might present from 9:00 to 10:00 on a Tuesday morning and then take questions. It was a good way to keep our company in front of the analysts, and we also had a quarterly phone call during which we released our earnings. That is now done via the web but in those days we conducted a conference call during which they could ask questions.

So we tried to give investors and advisors guidance and then they would add their own interpretation of our company's prospects. They would then share that information with their investment group or their shareholders. The primary concern was that they not float too far away from what we thought we were going to do. If they floated under, we let them float. But if they floated over, we became a little nervous. You might do what you think you can do or what you told them you could do, but you are still going to be taken down by the market if you come in under expectation.

I came to enjoy both the Wall Street and Washington visits. I always went with a professional and I had some training and practice at the podium to prepare. We did practice videos so I could see how I was doing. We went into depth on my presentations and worked hard with our internal department to develop them. Some may have not been the best presentations, but they were ones I could give. For instance, they would avoid inserting certain words that I never could pronounce. I really enjoyed working with Ray Caine, who headed our communications department. Once he said to me, "Jim, we are able to work around everything you say and cannot say, but you do know we are in the helicopter business. You can't keep saying *heelocopters.*" I had a lot of good people around me who would tell me if I was getting off base. Sometimes they did not tell me enough, but they tried.

There were certain things they insisted I do when making presentations to larger groups. For example, they liked seven-word sentences and told me to look up after every sentence. So we started working on that and then, of course, I became more at ease doing it. That helped more than anything and before long I came to enjoy giving the presentations.

For my New York visits we would fly in the helicopter directly to the Wall Street area. We might visit six offices in one day. It was really just making sales calls like I had done before, except now I was selling the company itself. I had to convince investors and advisors that we could overcome any problem that had come up because that is what they wanted to talk about. If my staff was able to anticipate the most difficult questions, the visits went much better.

I was never as comfortable in Washington as I was on Wall Street. That was probably because we were not promoting much except Bell Helicopter and the conversations inevitably revolved around the big experimental craft. But I went as needed, attended receptions, and shook hands and made small talk with members of Congress. We only had two representatives as well as the two senators from Rhode Island. I soon found it easiest to work with one of the representatives and Senator John Chafee.

At the time we were trying to maintain an operation in Turkey, and there was always a conflict in Congress as to whose side Turkey was really on. We had a venture in Turkey whereby we shipped them a partially completed helicopter and they completed it. We trained their workers on the helicopter assembly. So there was industry in Turkey and we got business out of it. Senator John Chafee would take me over to the House of Representatives and we would sit there in the early evening without anyone else around and he would talk about how Congress was run. He described how there could be one person who controlled maybe twenty votes. I later would sit in the House balcony and watch some of the proceedings.

My approach to representing Textron was to make sure people understood we were now a $14 billion corporation with over thirty companies. I realized there would always be some type of problem that I would have to manage. But with Textron's capabilities, most problems could be resolved satisfactorily and we had a history of doing just that.

Beverly Dolan once told me, "You have to have someone to help you because you can't have all these different pieces reporting to you. Someone needs to help you look after some of these operations." He thought, and the board agreed, that it should be an internal candidate. They certainly did not want to see me bring everybody with me from Emerson. I had no plans to do that even though I had no signed document prohibiting me from doing so. We promoted John S. Kleban from one of our larger units into a COO position. It turned out he had a serious problem with diabetes.

At Emerson we had to take a physical every year and reveal the results to the company, until it was determined this practice was not legal. To my knowledge, Textron had never required a physical so I had no idea about Kleban's health issue. We were going along pretty well into my second year and around March 1992, his wife called me on a Thursday to tell me he had pneumonia. He died the following Monday. I felt terrible for him and his family and it set us back somewhat at the company to have the COO position open again so soon. We began another internal search, and fortunately the company was doing well.

In our quest to add additional help we went to a Chicago search firm, the same one that had brought me to Textron, and looked at a number of candidates. Two people in the recruiting group really stood out, and one of them was almost a carbon copy of me. I kept hearing that MBA dictum that one must have a Mr. Inside and a Mr. Outside. Perhaps that was necessary on Wall Street and with that kind of work, but I was not going to go around the world making talks and giving seminars. So we went for the person we thought would add to the strategic and operational end. We hired Lewis Campbell in late 1992 as executive vice president and COO.

Campbell came to us from General Motors, where he had been the youngest person to be named vice president. He had been a real disciple and protégé of Robert C. Stemple, who had come to the end of his tour as chairman and CEO of General Motors. I suppose Lewis was looking around and once the headhunters started coming to him he showed interest in us and we hired him.

The Cessna acquisition in 1992 made the company much larger and prompted the idea that we had better hire some additional operational help. It also became apparent to the outside world that Textron was going to be a multi-industry, large cap stock. Acquiring Cessna would help us to move up to the top level.

We had moved ourselves into a position where we had some cash because we had made some major divestitures in the defense business. The financial sector knew we had some money, so when anything came up that had any size to it and was being auctioned off, meaning the parent company decides they are going to sell this business at the best price or deal they can get, they looked to Textron as a possible buyer.

Even though we had cash on hand, the size of Cessna meant we would also have to be willing to incur debt to make the purchase for what would be almost a $1 billion category purchase. Morgan Stanley was running the sale for Cessna. Boards will sometimes ask Goldman Sachs representatives to come in and tell you who out there could buy a particular company. We did that with Textron as we kept going up and up and our multiple did not quite come up as fast as our earnings. We kept looking behind us to see if somebody was going to take us over. Before long it got to the point that if that were to happen, it would have to be a GE or a company like United Technologies. There were very few companies that could afford to take over Textron.

If someone comes to your board and makes a public meaningful offer, the board must respond to it. The big question becomes, what is meaningful? Well, you cannot deny 25 or 30 percent above your stock price because that is pretty meaningful. And if you turn the offer down, your shareholders can ultimately force a sale. Our biggest protection probably was that we were a large multi-industry company. When we began selling off Speidel Watch Band and Homelite Chainsaw, we started narrowing down that multiple gap a little bit more. But fortunately we got to be expensive before the cash accumulated and the gap came down.

Cessna was a pure auction, which meant we had to do the best job of going to visit the company, listen to them make their management presentation, and then make an offer to Morgan Stanley. At that point companies always started doing all the things you would expect, like saying, "You'd better go look again" or "We've got another bid that is higher." They would attempt to get the number of serious buyers down to two or three and, in the case of Cessna, they had three. We did not know who the other two prospective buyers were; in one case, we would never have guessed the name of the buyer. It turned out to be an attempted takeover by management.

I remember one Sunday in 1992 receiving a call from Morgan Stanley in which the representative said, "Believe it or not, three people have made the same offer, $585 million." I called several people, including Beverly Dolan and one of his close associates on the board, and told them, "I'm flying to Charlotte tomorrow morning so let's talk this over." After a lot of discussion we decided the obvious move was to go to $600 million, so we should offer $620 million. We bought Cessna for $620 million.

I urged throwing the purchase number out on the table because I thought we could justify the amount to Wall Street, which was my responsibility. If the others had said no, I would not have done it because I did not have that authority. I was already on thin ice because I had only gone to two board members out of the twelve about the offer. But the board had given management an opportunity to take another look. They never put a cap on us, but I had been around long enough to know it was always best to talk to somebody on the board instead of just throwing it out there and then going back and saying, "Well, you gave me an okay." In this case, I had two other people who were with me and they were both very important to the board.

The announcement that we had purchased Cessna came out about three days later. I still have the *Wall Street Journal* article because it was the only time a caricature of me appeared in the press. The article said, "This guy came in from Emerson Electric and we knew he had the background for managing operations and he had been doing a good job with this company. Now he goes out and spends money like a drunken sailor."

To make it an even bigger story, which did not get into the *Wall Street Journal,* the next week we had scheduled a meeting with Textron's division presidents in Atlanta. I invited Russ Meyer, the president of Cessna, to make the same presentation about Cessna to the division presidents that he had made to me during the negotiations. As he walked into the room I went over to greet him. Before I could even shake his hand he said, "Hello, Jim, I just want you to know I'll be leaving within three months." I later learned he was very upset that they had lost the internal management takeover bid.

In many ways Meyer was Cessna, and he was a company legend. He was very good on his feet and seemingly known by everyone. He was an excellent golfer and close friends with Arnold Palmer. All I said to Meyer that day was, "Well, we'll see what we can work out. I'd like for you to meet some of our people." I had no assurance I could change his mind but I knew from that day forward I had to try to keep him.

I will never forget when I went out to Wichita to meet with Meyer and review some mockups and other details. Meyer could be somewhat arrogant and made a point of not meeting with appointments in his office, which is also a Walmart practice, or at least it used to be. If you went to Walmart to sell something, they met you in the lobby. Off the lobby were small meeting rooms with just a table and a couple of chairs. The room was bare otherwise—not even a wastepaper basket.

Somehow Meyer concluded that I could generate enough money to help Cessna grow and he admitted as much to me later. But during our first few meetings he talked extensively about Cessna, the company's importance, and what it meant to the aviation world. At times it seemed Russ was really more interested in letting me know what *he* meant to the aviation world. Finally, after hearing enough, I said, "Russ, you know, I think I have an ego about as big as yours. I think I know how to operate things and I know how to generate what's needed for operations. I see no reason why we can't use your expertise, knowledge, background, and reputation. I will get the resources you need to build Cessna the way you envision. After that, you can make your decision about staying or leaving. Unless you've got something you absolutely know you want to do in life, why don't you stay here? I know you love Cessna."

Meyer told me he would consider it. After thinking about it, he decided he wanted a contract and I gave him one. The contract allowed him to fly airplanes, even into retirement, as long as he, obviously, stayed certified. My thinking was why wouldn't we want him to fly? He could fly out to meet with a prospective customer at Pebble Beach and probably have a better chance of making a sale than anyone else within the company. I had seen him conduct business and knew what he could do for us.

After we worked everything out, I never had any other conflicts with Russ. I never really tried to bluff people. I just told them exactly what I saw and I tried to know what they were thinking. The key to the acquisition for Meyer was that we could put Cessna in a better position to fund what he wanted to do. I never thought it was any love for me or any great friendship that kept him on board.

In a management takeover a management team decides they want to take a company private. In other words, they will buy it off the stock market. A company does the same thing. When we paid the $620 million for Cessna, a certain portion of the money went to the shareholders, particularly the portion that was above the value of the General Dynamics stock.

Internal people attempting to purchase a company have to find investors who will go with them. Perhaps they put some of their own money in it, but when you run it up against a number like $600 million, you cannot expect to have somebody sitting there on the management team with that type of wealth or they would not be working there every day. So they had gone out and secured banks and investors to come up with the money. If not, Morgan Stanley would not even have considered them.

When a company is purchased one expects change. When somebody puts down $620 million and picks up some goodwill to put on their books, they have to find some way to show rapid improvement in either growth or earnings. For example, we had an item we thought could be used by Cessna. We knew that at one time they had been in single-engine, propeller aircraft production that used engines like the ones we made.

There are always plusses and minuses to these types of purchases. I am sure somebody in 2009 said, "My God, Cessna's not doing very well now so I wish it hadn't happened." But Cessna had seventeen good years before the economic downturn. The combination of people not spending money in 2008–2009 and the government making a rather strong case against private planes at corporations drove the downturn. You cannot expect all buyers to be like my friend down in Tennessee who can purchase one by himself. So the corporate world drives the market or the share situation, like NetJets and those types of enterprises. Textron still owns Cessna and it still has a real value. Its strong value helps support the Textron stock price. It probably does not have as much in earnings as it did at one time but it has come back. It was not doing well in 1991 and that helped us some with the purchase price.

We needed Cessna's size and we were already in the aviation business with Bell Helicopter. We were up in the air, so to speak, and we probably anticipated more synergy between Cessna and Bell than ever developed. But we did fill that void in a big way. The whole run of the stock going up as much as it did in the 1990s would not have happened without Cessna.

Emerson had a Falcon airplane that I had flown in many times. When I went to Textron we had a Challenger, a Falcon, and a Cessna Citation. So I had not been exposed enough to how strong Cessna was and how strong they were going to become.

We had a couple of things happen early on that really helped the price we paid for Cessna. One of the major sizes, the Citation 7, was to be phased out. But then suddenly NetJets—at that time they were called Executive Jet—decided to expand into Europe. So they purchased a bunch of Citation 7s to start their European wing and that purchase kept the model going a little longer. We had a large cargo-type plane that was used a lot in Alaska for fishing trips or to haul cargo into rather remote areas because it could be configured to land on water. That plane was supposed to be phased out but it is still in use today because companies like UPS are picking it up for their smaller runs. So there were a lot of things happening that helped cover any shortfall we had in our own business plan.

I liked Cessna as a company from the start. It exuded class that you could sense when you walked into their headquarters. Cessna became one of my five favorite companies. The other companies in my top five have a much lower public profile.

I keep a few of the Cessna models on display in my office to this day. I suppose I have always been very interested in the idea of getting up in the morning and getting two or three important visits completed by the end of the day. I am a firm believer that using airplanes for corporate travel is the same as using one's car. How would you like to run a company if you did not have an automobile? The way we used our planes was not to fly to the Bahamas for the weekend, but we moved people around and, I think, justified their costs.

We had other good businesses but they were not growing as

fast as Cessna. The Cessna growth was based not just on corporate sales but on the idea that one could buy a share of an airplane. There are now five or six of those types of companies. You can buy a quarter of an airplane or a sixteenth of an airplane and you sign an agreement that says you will allow other people to use your sixteenth and you will get to use all the similar type airplanes that this company operates. So you may never see the airplane's tail number listed on your Subchapter S. I may never see the two tail numbers I am flying and paying for, but I will be flying a similar plane in terms of age, size, and model.

One of the keys to success is getting out to the various operations. Sitting in the office and waiting for people to come to you does not work. You have got to get on that "visiting court" and that is something I really enjoyed doing. I like to visit the plants and see people where they work. We always operated that way with our five-year planning cycle. We would go to their location and sit with them and listen to them in their home environment as they made a presentation. They could have just as well have piled everything in a briefcase and come to us, but it was far better going to them. If they wanted to show you something that was in a demonstration room or if they wanted to take you down to the plant, you were there. So that was key and fortunately we were in a good economic period. The 1990s were a great time.

We took advantage of the improved economy and going global, which can mean two things. You can say you are global if you buy all your materials from around the world or you can say you are global if you sell your products around the world. When we first began going global, we started buying materials internationally and we picked up a competitive situation for the American market. Maybe steel was hurt by that, but we were not exactly taking machinery and other items to be built outside the US. There was something coming in and we were still doing manufacturing in the US during the 1990s. It became a gradual process whereby we moved out more and more manufacturing until it begins to hurt American manufacturing. So I was lucky enough to be in that balance situation. It is a little different story now.

I had a great colleague, Herb Henkel, who later became CEO of Ingersoll Rand. He essentially headed the industrial segment while I focused more on Cessna, and Lewis Campbell focused on the finance companies and Bell, even though the organizational structure did not show that. Henkel was from Austria, could speak several languages, and was comfortable around the world.

Henkel and I traveled many miles on airplanes going somewhere to look at something. Then we started picking off locations and buying companies. I remember one company in the automotive sector, which Textron still owns, that made plastic fuel tanks and operated in fifteen countries. That helped us become more international and Henkel was very helpful with his understanding of international business.

We were not in a position to operate like General Electric did in those days. GE would send forty or fifty people to China and that is no exaggeration. They would look over the market and eventually find some niche they wanted to enter. If you could afford to do it that way it probably offered the most return in the long run. But we had to be very careful that we made acquisitions that were on a solid footing.

For example, we made acquisitions in Brazil. If you buy something in Brazil expecting that economy to be steady and to carry you for a number of years, you would be wrong. So we bought a facility there that had extra capacity and we moved our operation into the facility. Our theory in regard to this particular product line was we would design it, research it, get it right, and get it four or five years down the road in the marketplace. Then we would offload it into the Brazil facility and bring in new products to feed the US facility. We knew we had capacity but I am not sure if we knew it would work as well as it did or if we could find enough new products to keep the US production facilities going. But that approach worked well.

If you were a CEO of a Fortune 100 company in the middle of the 1990s and you could not say in your annual report that you had been to China, you were probably in trouble. It did not matter if you simply went to China to see the Great Wall and tour the country. We were all going to China then because we knew we should be there.

I first went to China with Textron in 1993. When I was with Emerson we went to China to look at a manufacturing site and eventually opened a plant in south China near Hong Kong. But I had never really been there just to look at China. When I first went to China you could not find anyone from the US who was making any money. I remember being at a session with GE about their lamp division, which was lightbulbs. The lamp division had been there for a long time and still they were not making any money.

In those days, especially with the American car companies, you generally worked with a Chinese partner. You took them a model to design and they made the model and sold it. But you could not establish a partnership without the Chinese government's approval and the Chinese government more or less directed you. In those days China wanted automotive companies in a lot of different locations in most of the provinces. We went to China mainly with Volkswagen to make plastic fuel tanks for them.

I always felt I had a deficiency in international business that I never entirely overcame. For example, a Kentucky accent can be very difficult for an interpreter. So I always felt I lacked in this area and that is probably why I relied so heavily on Herb. Some people could just shift into different languages with ease. I talked on the phone with the young CEO from WABCO, who could easily shift from one language to another. He seemed to learn to adjust to my accent. But I was always interested in knowing the customs of the various countries. For example, when we first went to China we hired an outside firm to come and sit with us the first morning and tell us some of the things to avoid in our body language, motions, or words. This proved to be extremely helpful in our meetings and interactions. I found I had to make many more adjustments beyond getting used to a different time zone and local food.

I was really big on hiring local managers rather than sending someone in from the outside. If I could find managers who had experience working with US companies and I could bring them over into our company, it usually worked out pretty well. On the other hand, it was hard to just pick someone up who had been working in China or Japan all their life with Chinese or Japanese companies. But if I found somebody who had the right background, and I often did, I hired them.

Of all the countries I dealt with I probably felt least safe in Thailand and sometimes Mexico, depending on where we were in the country. Brazil, particularly Rio de Janeiro, was pretty tough as well. It has probably gotten more dangerous in some of those locations. George Thomas handled our security but we did not take our own security with us. George arranged for local security wherever we traveled.

I did not give much thought to kidnapping back then, and Textron never had a problem. Of course, we knew of other companies who had people kidnapped and held for ransom. I did not know the individuals but I knew it could happen. I knew someday we might have to make a decision as to whether we paid or not, but fortunately I never had to make that call. We understood that, just as in parts of this country, there were certain hours of the day when one should not to be running around in some places. When our Textron group traveled into questionable areas we kept everything pretty wrapped up.

As a younger man going to Japan in 1969 and 1970 and wanting to be a good guest, I would occasionally find myself in a situation where the hosts attempted to take me to questionable places. I always had to come up with a good excuse not to go. Of course, there were some people prone to those activities and they developed reputations. They had a tendency to "over entertain." I thought it best to simply avoid those situations. I do not think I have ever been labeled "a real party guy."

During my time at Textron we decreased defense and financials and picked up on industrial products like Cessna. The company had begun selling off consumer business when I arrived and we continued that practice. Something I would advise anyone about business—although probably not everyone would agree—is that it is best to look at a business on a five-year basis. Every year you look at the next five years. Either that business gives you a return, you find something to acquire to help it, or you sell it.

Perhaps I gave up on some businesses a little quicker than I should have. I would not allow a business to hold us down if we did not have a plan for it to succeed. Fortunately, the board usually agreed with my plans. I took a couple of issues before the board more than once to get it done. On a couple of other occasions the board did not agree with me. They thought my plan was just too risky or the return number was not high enough. I remember one instance when a board of one of our companies in London disappointed me by not backing one of my plans. But the advantage of running a multi-industry operation is I could simply work with another part of the company that might give us the same good outcome.

There were a couple of instances when division leaders would get a financial person to side with them and they would fix the books to cover their story. When that happened, I often discovered it when it was too late and the financials they reported were incorrect. Sometimes we took a real and unexpected financial hit. Obviously, we had to remove these people from their positions.

If we needed to make some financial adjustments and I had enough time, I would call Russ at Cessna and ask, "Russ, can you ship a couple more planes this quarter?" Then I would call Webb Joyner at Bell and ask, "How about helping us out here?" Russ Meyer and Webb Joyner, like all of our managers, held options on Textron stock so they were motivated to help. Back then we used accruals a lot more. Now it is illegal to hold back anything. That is not to say it was something we did that no one else did. But if you went down that path and your profits were a little bit stronger than you thought they would be, you could look at restructuring plans, something you might do down the road in the future, and you could set up an accrual for that. And then, a year later, you could decide whether or not to do it because the market had changed or you had to have a justification. Today, whatever you see is what a company has. That is probably better because it prevents companies from reserving something they really do not need.

I mentioned earlier that Textron sold off our insurance businesses. I found this process to be very interesting. We put Paul Revere insurance out with its own stock on the New York Stock Exchange. Paul Revere was one of four NYSE companies I chaired until we sold it to Provident. In this case we did not simply go out and say it was for sale like we did with Avco Finance.

Textron's Commercial Finance Division was a very good business while I was there. I will not attempt here to analyze what happened after I left because I do not know all of the details. Suffice it to say, I would never have let them expand outside of our Textron products. It was utilized by Textron to finance Bell Helicopters, E-Z-GO golf carts, Jacobsen turf care equipment, and Cessna. Cessna had a different branch but it was lumped into the Textron Commercial Finance Division.

During the 1990s, when everyone aspired to be an entrepreneur and was doing a lot of investing, we were cutting out finance transactions. It just did not make sense to me to suddenly balloon this thing up because I did not think Wall Street could read which way Textron was going. For example, why is it so bad to have insurance and consumer loans if it is so great to have commercial loans? Then, after the turndown in the early 2000s as we started having this spurt up until 2007–2008, the new group, which had become more financial-oriented than I was, went out and did a lot of loans of other types. Now they are trying to write those loans down and sell them, and that is why the stock is not performing very well.

I learned this lesson from Emerson. Westinghouse decided they were going to go very heavy into financials as early as the

1980s. Their stock was probably just jumping. GE did the same thing. Emerson's stock was not jumping that way, but did we need to buy a finance company? No. Emerson decided not to buy the company and that probably had a lot to do with my reluctance later. I find that finance companies are hard to manage because they have one thing in mind and that is revenue growth. The whole theory was if you can get enough of the top line you could absorb your costs and you would be fine. The problem is, you load that cost there to support big revenue, and if revenue goes down you are stuck.

Nevertheless, it was very tempting. The Textron stock when I left was at $80. It went to $117 or $118. So the person who bought at $80 and sold at $117 would think Textron's management team the best in the world. Whereas the guy who bought at $117 and then watched the price dip to $20 might feel different about management. I should add for accuracy that Textron stock split and that took it down to $60 before it later fell to $20.

I have discussed both Emerson's and Textron's international expansion. Most discussions about today's public policy and the economy generally included the benefits of the North American Free Trade Act and other similar trade agreements. These types of agreements are usually questioned in regards to their impact on employment and wages. Increasingly, companies have relocated manufacturing operations outside the United States. Perhaps more could have been done with tax incentives to keep them here. The only place to increase taxes was on business and many wondered why that could not be done. It was a very popular idea. The average voter did not care if you raised taxes on business as long as they themselves did not have to pay more taxes. Moreover, the average voter just wanted cheap electronics and other consumer products.

It might have been possible to find ways to stimulate business leaders to create more jobs in the US by tax incentives, but I am just not sure. We have become a research economy that is still very innovative, but we send our products to be made elsewhere.

The automobile companies like Toyota are building cars in the US at competitive prices, and they are not burdened with old pension plans and are usually not unionized. They started from scratch and they were in a twenty-year plan. They are not any smarter than we are but they learned from what happened to American car companies.

One has to first put some thought into what it means to be competitive in an international economy. It is not the easiest thing to do to buy a television from China to put on American store shelves. You have to have a very specialized group of people to watch the quality and do the negotiations. Then you have to put it on a ship and send it to the US. So you have all that inventory in transit and coming in, and you have to have more inventory because you cannot expect quick turnarounds. I sometimes wonder if the worm is not going to eventually turn to where China raises their wages enough and freight costs increase to the point that there will be some back-feeding into these plants in the US.

I do not know when it will impact televisions because we have allowed the technology to go offshore, and foreign manufacturers are the ones who have introduced flat screens and other new technologies. I think the day will come when we will have pretty strong manufacturing of WABCO products and systems in this country because the people making these trucks see so much fluctuation in the demand. They want very quick service and do not want to hold the inventory.

I believe the only thing that will correct this situation is for them to start over-costing. Now where are you going to run next? I remember in the 1970s we put a buying group in Belgium because we could buy materials in Europe less expensively than in the United States. Then we looked at putting plants in Ireland because we got a tax holiday there. Emerson eventually operated three plants in that country. Then we began looking seriously at Taiwan, China, India, and the Philippines. We were a little more hesitant about Thailand and Indonesia because of security and stability issues. We never considered Australia because of the cost. Finally, one had to be a really wild thinker or a huge risk taker to even consider going to the Middle East.

I do not believe Americans realize how much money there would be to spend in this country if it were not for all the wars we are involved in around the globe. I get so upset when I read about people in other countries who do not like Americans. I am sure they have their reasons because we have more money, we generally live better, and we can be arrogant. But the United States is protecting the free world. Moreover, we supply more humanitarian aid around the world than any other country by far.

If we discover a cure for cancer, it will not be long before we put the cure in the international arena. The pharmaceutical companies get beat up because they charge so much for their products while you can bring them in from Canada or somewhere else cheaper. Well, the other countries do not have to pay for the research. Generally, I am very positive about our future and I do not think we are like the Roman Empire. I do wish we would not spend quite so much government money so quickly because it takes time to understand the impact in most cases.

In regard to healthcare generally, my whole background says we have to lower the costs. If you have a program that does not lower the cost at the same time you put more money in, the user will absorb the need for money, but there will not be a lower cost. I would put the money into the things that would help the most. For example, many of our hospitals have become outdated. We have rural hospitals that need our help. Maybe we don't have enough highly trained physicians. But I personally do not understand the approach of trying to insure everyone.

I am not opposed to scales on taxes. I never really understood why I should not pay taxes. I am never too upset when there is going to be a tax increase for people who make over a certain dollar amount, whatever that number is. Like many Americans with wealth, my greatest concern is how the government uses the money. I do not think members of Congress who want to spend that money understand how aggravating it is for a person who has earned the money, and has made it possible for lots of other people to earn money, to just watch that money being frittered away.

If I were in a position to do something about taxes, I would go to the wealthy, however "wealthy" is determined, and say, "I'm going to raise your taxes, but I'm going to cut out the estate taxes." I mean, that is dual taxation. Eliminating the estate tax might not help me much during my lifetime, but one has to consider one's children and grandchildren. The idea that I am going to be taxed at 45 percent, again, is just fine with me. My family will be fine. But it just seems a little unusual. I think I could explain to the wealthy, those making over $250,000, that my plan would be a pretty good trade-off.

Also, we have to incentivize our workforce to get more education and job training. I have followed this issue, and one of the problems we face is we could retrain you but we cannot guarantee you a place to work where you want to live. You must be willing to move for the retraining to really pay off. You might say, "Let's train Jim Hardymon to use a computer and then he'll have other outlets in Lexington, Kentucky." Well, I understand that, but if you are just trying to take a welder and you are going to train them to be head of a distribution center in Des Moines, they have to move to Des Moines. A few years back we were going through a plant closing in one of my Investcorp companies when I served on the board. We planned to expand one of our other plants and when we talked to the employees about moving to the other plant, about two hundred miles away, most would not move. In one way it was better for us because we did not have to pay as much severance, but we would have preferred it if the employees had been willing to relocate because they were already trained. It would also have been better for the employees because they would not have had to go through a period of unemployment. Understand that is coming from someone who moved fourteen times during the course of his career.

In most discussions about the modern development of Textron, I get credit for evolving it from a classic holding company to an operating company, building and growing business-es. The board supported me in doing that because we delivered consistent growth over thirty-seven consecutive quarters, with the earnings going from 70 cents to $2.68 a share between 1989 and 1998. I also get credit for bringing in the first-ever operations management process, although my predecessors would probably not agree with that. I think Textron is still using the same process today.

I always thought I had to be hands-on and bring discipline to the process. I know I can seem boring and I am sure people in the company wondered often, "Is he going to talk about process and discipline again?" We had to stay with that process no matter what we were doing. Whether we were working with golf carts, airplanes, or finance, we benefited from staying with the process, even though in some cases it had to be slightly modified. I really believed that. Chuck Knight, my mentor at Emerson, always said, "If it's not simple it isn't going to work." He also told us, "If you're going somewhere to do something, get there the night before."

So at Textron we leveraged our collective strengths and syn-ergies. We acquired companies with complementary products, markets, or manufacturing processes and capabilities. Each com-ponent could not change that much by its own growth. Change came through acquisitions. But we could not do the acquisitions if we did not have the cash on hand. So we sold off certain busi-nesses to raise the necessary cash.

Putting too much into the automotive section of Textron was probably a mistake because it was based on the success of GM, Ford, and Chrysler. We had $1 billion with Chrysler and we were riding a real tired horse. I knew Chrysler was in trouble because they became increasingly hard to deal with. GM brought in a man from Spain named Jose Ignacio Lopez and he would just look at a contract like it was not there. So, here we had our plant geared up, our people geared up to make this product, and suddenly he an-nounces, "I don't care what that contract says. You're going to give it to me for this price, and you're going to wait this long to get your money or you've got to shut your plant down and I'll just send it somewhere else." When they began that type of behavior I knew they were wrong. Nevertheless, the last thing we sold off were automotive items. I went to Europe a couple times in the last month I was at Textron because we were having a hard time getting that divestiture closed due to the requirement to get permission from the regulatory groups. I stayed on a little longer than I would have just because of this.

Actually, as long as we had Chrysler working with us as a partner it was a pretty good business. But who would ever have thought Chrysler would be sold off to a foreign company or that General Motors, one of the most respected companies in the world, would start violating contracts? The automotive problems began before I left, and my only regret is that I did not have enough time to make the divestiture and find another acquisition.

At Textron we moved employees around frequently. We set up a human resources room, or an organization room that we kept very private. We had high-potential employees, people over sixty years old, and employees who were not doing as well as we needed them to do. We had this all laid out in different segments.

If someone came to us and said, "I need somebody in human resources," the way the room was built, we could go in and focus on the good human resource people. You could see all the information, and our people could then give you resumes, bios, compensation, whatever you wanted. And then we would go to the person they were working for and we would say, "Look, this person can get a better job. You're going to have to let them interview. If it wasn't a better job, I would not be supporting this. We'll bring you in the room and find somebody down the list to bring up if you don't have an internal solution." It worked well for the most part. Some managers hid their good people or otherwise tried to shield them from moving. They would have a project that just had to be completed in the next six months and if they did not have this particular person it would not get done.

The whole idea of cross-training in manufacturing was to put in what we called cells. So instead of having a product where you stamped out the fitting here and you sent it somewhere else to be plated and somewhere else to be boxed, we created these cells. We would buy the equipment that would level out the capacity. So if you wanted to make 150 an hour, the machines were geared to make 150 an hour. You did not have some press over here that could do 550. Then all the people working in there, which might only be eight to fifteen, were cross-trained so they could do every process in that cell. That would cut down on boredom and on problems with absenteeism.

We had plants in Los Angeles that nobody could afford to live within forty or fifty miles of. Workers were probably spending over two hours on the road each day. So we changed the work schedule to four ten-hour days instead of having them go home after an eight-hour day only to sleep and then return. We created a schedule whereby they got to have three full days off, although not everybody got Fridays and Saturdays. In Michigan we found we had high absenteeism on the first day of hunting season. So we told our employees they would not get off President's Day, but they could have off the first day of hunting season. We had good human resources people.

Looking back at managing a multi-faceted, complex organization, it seems easier in retrospect than it did at the time. I may have made it sound a little bit easier than it was. Every problem might not have gotten fixed the first time around, but we worked on problems until they were solved.

We used to take our annual meeting on the road when other companies had theirs at the same place each year. Most people try to hide their annual meetings, but with the success we had with ours, we did not have to hide. Once we held the meeting in Rockford, Illinois, where we had three different plants. We had no idea how many retirees might show up. So many people tried to come into the meeting room we had to set up televisions in adjoining rooms. When we went to Bell Helicopter we had a tremendous turnout. People were interested in the company and many of them owned some stock and it worked out well.

Upon reflection, I am amazed at how fast my time at Textron flew by. I found the work challenging and I enjoyed the opportunity to prove I could run a large company successfully. I was pleased we raised the company's value substantially and the components were in good shape. But I was approaching sixty-five years old and I had agreed to stay with Textron until then. I knew change was coming.

Chapter Five

"Retirement"

Deciding when to retire can be very tricky.
Some people in the company tell you
to stay even when they would really like
for you to leave. Others really do want you to stay
because they know that a change at the top
can cause widespread disruptions throughout the company.

I believe retirement is one of the most important transitions a person makes. As I approached retirement, I had just experienced one of the most successful decades of my entire career. I must give some credit to a robust US economy at the time, but we had Textron poised to benefit from an economic upturn. During that successful run I thought back to the people I had worked with during my career who had contributed to my success. I suggest anybody who wants to achieve, and perhaps even do more than they think they can, should gather around them mentors and people who will offer support when needed.

My grandfather and father served as my first mentors without even realizing it. Even though neither my grandfather nor my father had shared much with me about the world of work and business, they impacted me tremendously. My grandfather Hardymon probably never spoke two sentences to me about the family business. But as I think about the time I spent with him, there is something almost mysterious about how much I learned from him. Likewise, my father was known in the community as a hard worker who was thorough, trustworthy, and honest. He and I likewise never spoke much about business. He operated in a different world: of farming, tobacco production, and small businesses. But Dad's values made an impression on me that I did not fully appreciate until later in life.

When I first entered the world of large businesses and corporations, Frank Jones convinced me to take my first job with Browning Manufacturing. As a mentor, he demonstrated to me the values of promptness, preparation, and making the extra effort. Everybody recognized and appreciated those traits in Frank.

After Emerson Electric acquired Browning Manufacturing, Larry Browning became my champion. Without his recommendation I seriously doubt that anyone at Emerson would have picked me out of the ranks of a little Maysville company to take on more responsibility. There is no doubt in my mind that Larry made the difference. Then, at Emerson, Chuck Knight vaulted me into important experiences that helped me be successful at Emerson and later at Textron. So I credit several people over the course of my life and career who helped me be successful.

I faced retirement at a time when it seemed that corporate leaders were retiring earlier than ever before. I began contemplating retirement when I turned sixty-two. I understood that planning discussions within the company are about topics and strategies that I would not likely be there to implement. That makes it hard to get excited about the discussions when you realize you will not have any role in their implementation. Of all the boards and companies that I have been associated with, I do not remember anybody except Chuck Knight working until the age of sixty-five. People choose to get out because they had made some wealth and because, as one rises higher in the chain of command, it becomes an increasingly tougher business.

Deciding when to retire can be very tricky. Some people in the company tell you to stay even when they would really like for you to leave. Others really do want you to stay because they know that a change at the top can cause widespread disruptions throughout the company. The Textron board and I had an understanding that I would leave in 1999 because all my incentives were based on me retiring at sixty-five.

The months leading up to my retirement were a little confusing because I stepped out of the CEO position to become chairman of Textron. Lewis B. Campbell, who had been with Textron for seven years, was my obvious successor and became CEO. But once I became chairman, it was inevitable that Wall Street, our employees, and everyone else gravitated away from me and towards the CEO. In retrospect, it would have been best if I had gone to a non-executive chairmanship. I convinced a board I served on later to handle their transition that way. A non-executive is only involved with the board meetings and occasionally a special situation in which a customer or employee contact wants their help. But at Textron, for me to hang around and basically have another job created for me became somewhat awkward.

At the beginning of the transition, Campbell and I sat down and agreed on what my responsibilities would be as chairman. But before too long, it became obvious to me that I could not do my job because he had all of the authority. We did not part on bad terms but we both understood that the arrangement was not working. I had planned to participate in Textron's March 1999 annual meeting, but after the January board meeting we pulled the plug on that by mutual consent. I would be less than candid if I did not say that, considering the incentives I would receive at age sixty-five, I was not going to be the one to suggest that I leave the company any earlier. But the board settled with me to my satisfaction and without any conflict. Fortunately, I did not lose any of my guaranteed compensation. As it turned out, the timing was very beneficial because shortly after I left, Textron's stock value began to fluctuate. I had no plans for what I might do in retirement, but I knew I was not the type of person who could retire and do nothing. The end of my board service seemed to be fast approaching as I neared retirement because nearly every New York Stock Exchange board placed age limits on their board members. At some point, the age limit for serving on boards moved from seventy-two to seventy-five. But several things occurred that made the two decades after retirement as important to me as the decade prior to it.

The first board I ever served on was the Emerson Electric Board, on which I served as an employee. But Emerson believed strongly that only the CEO could be on outside boards, whereas Textron believed that serving on other boards offers knowledge that helps you manage your own board better and might even provide insights to use in your business.

At Textron I first went on the Fleet Bank Board, mostly because it was tradition as both companies were located in Providence. Fortunately, when I joined the bank board I was placed on the compensation committee, which I chaired for a number of years. I served on this committee because I did not know banking. I could not have contributed much any other way, but that worked out well for me.

Later the Textron Board urged me to join another industrial-type board, so I went on the Air Products and Chemicals Inc. Board. It is a great company that focuses primarily on industrial gases and is the largest manufacturer of hydrogen in the world. I did learn things at Air Products that I was able to bring back to Textron. Boards have to be careful and also be reminded periodically for whom they are working; the shareholders, not the CEO. Sometimes boards want to pacify the CEO and be in on everything to the extent that they begin thinking the wrong way. Air Products was very shareholder-oriented and I brought that knowledge away from my service on their board.

At the time I moved from CEO to chairman of Textron, one of my board members was very involved in Schneider Electric, a French company. He talked me into going on their board, where I served for seven years. Schneider is very similar to Emerson in that it supplies components. Schneider had bought an American company, Square D, before I joined the board in the late 1990s. They wanted one US citizen on the board and I was it. Of the sixteen board members, twelve were from Paris, one from England, one from Germany, one from Italy, and me. The Englishman on the board knew some French but he also needed help with the language so they constructed a room behind some glass next to the board room where the interpreters sat and spoke to the Englishman and me through headphones. Everybody had a microphone. If you wanted to speak you pushed the button on your microphone until the red light came on so the interpreters could hear the meeting conversations. One of the worst things about working through an interpreter is when somebody says something that the interpreter does not hear. The interpreter then says, "You're going to have to tell them I can't hear." Then you interrupt the entire meeting. But overall it worked well.

The distributed printed matter came in English. When I went on the board the CEO said he thought the board would soon be an English-speaking board. Well, he misjudged that entirely because the French were not about to accept that. I attended six board meetings a year for seven years. I primarily focused on the relationship between Schneider and Square D. During that time I got to know Charles Denny at Square D really well and we remain friends today. Even though they have age limits, they asked me to continue because half of the board can be over the age limit. I liked serving on that board, but I did not want to sign on for another six years.

As it turned out, the real reward for me in retirement was the ability to serve on eleven different New York Stock Exchange boards. I did not approach retirement thinking I would be just as busy as before, but I had considered the possibility of serving on boards. I was not sure I would even be asked to serve but I soon began receiving several requests for board work. A recruiter contacted me about working with Investcorp, an investment company chaired by a person who actually has his office in Bahrain. He created this group of investors and the company goes out and buys businesses. For example, we had a ladder company and packaging companies but not much pure manufacturing. We acquired mostly service-type companies.

By the time my board service with Investcorp ended in November 2015, I had served on six of their boards. And contrary to the type of stock option I had with the corporate world, where you could exercise your stock options, there was no way to do that with Investcorp. Their stock had no value until the company was sold because it was not on the New York Stock Exchange or any other stock exchange. The stock was merely a paper you had that indicated you owned a certain percentage of the company and you received that percentage when it sold. In reality, each stockholder was a part owner. It was set up that way because the goal was to grow the companies and sell them. They were flipping those companies and had no desire to keep them very long.

In most cases, Investcorp kept the same management team that was in place at the time they purchased a company. Most of the companies had strong family ownership so Investcorp would buy out the families and, in some cases, leave a portion of the ownership with the family. Most often, the family would keep running the business because they had the ties to the customer. Investcorp would then create a board comprised mostly of its own employees. I served on the Investcorp boards as one of the few independent directors.

The last board I served on for Investcorp was a packaging company that was sold in 2015. I suppose if they had not sold it I would have stayed longer. But I knew it was getting to be time. The board met often as the CEO of the company wanted the board to help with customers. We often held board meetings at customer locations so we could see their business and how they were using our packaging product. Plus, it gave the board members the opportunity to get to know the CEO better. But it required a great deal more travel than I wanted at that point, so I decided that was a good time to step aside. Overall, Investcorp proved to be a very fulfilling opportunity for me at that point in my life.

Two boards asked me to serve at the same time: American Standard and Circuit City. I felt very much at home on the American Standard Board since they were manufacturing. At that time they had an abnormally large number of insiders on the board. They had probably been brought together by the CEO, but he was facing retirement. There was a three-member committee of the board charged with starting the search for a new CEO, whether in-house or from outside. They were also charged with reconfiguring the board and looking at a business that was pretty foreign to the other industrial businesses they had. It was more in the medical field. The committee eventually brought back to the board a recommendation to divest, which they did. So I came in on the ground floor while the longtime CEO was still there, and I was the first of the new wave they brought in as directors.

While on the American Standard Board I got to know Dan Quayle extremely well. He also served on the board. I had met Quayle earlier because he was very willing to give his time to visit with the Textron Board, which met in Washington quite often. He came as a guest. He would sit with the board, join us for dinner, and make some remarks. I did not know him very well during my time at Textron because he was mainly oriented to the people at our Washington office. But as I got to know him better on the American Standard Board, I really enjoyed our friendship.

American Standard is headquartered in Piscataway, New Jersey, and Quayle and I were the only out-of-towners at the board meetings. We stayed at an Embassy Suites about a block and a half from the American Standard offices. Before long, after a board dinner, we would often return to the hotel and sit in the bar and talk. We would usually meet the next morning for breakfast and walk over to the meeting together. Sometimes we shared a ride to the airport. So through all of that I got to know him fairly well. I remember he was a great sports fan.

When George H. W. Bush chose Dan as his running mate in 1988 I was concerned that he was being over-promoted. I thought that if he had remained a US senator he would have become a great senior senator. Notwithstanding any spelling errors or other mistakes they hung on him, he is very smart. His is also an internationalist and really understands the international scene. The opportunity to be vice president came along rather unexpectedly. He could have remained a junior senator for a while longer and worked his way up in seniority. In my opinion, if he had stayed in office he would have made a big difference for Indiana and for the country.

Over the years I have met a lot of people. But as time goes by I obviously tend to remember more about the people with whom I spent the most time. My children and grandchildren think I know someone wherever we go. When I think of my friends, like Larry Bossidy, Jack Welch, and Chuck Knight, I recall the tough times we worked through together. I have not forgotten and neither have they. To this day, if something comes up and I need their help, I know I can call them and they will answer. I can count on their friendship even if we have not seen one another for months or even years. I consider Dan Quayle to be one of those friends.

Senator Bob Dole was another good political contact over the years. Of course, we had the Cessna operation in Wichita with a lot of employees. I spent a fair amount of time with him during his run for the presidency and afterwards because of our mutual interest in treating and curing prostate cancer. After my experience with prostate cancer, I became more involved in fundraising for UK's Urology Department and Senator Dole helped secure some additional funds for the UK Medical Center.

Senator Dole's presidential campaign was very similar to Senator John McCain's later run for the presidency. The Republicans knew they had tried and true members of the party they wanted to honor—and in my opinion, they did not think they had much of a chance of winning the general election. I do not think any other Republican candidate could have won either of those elections.

American Standard is now gone because we sold the bath and kitchen manufacturing and before I went off the board, we spun out what is called WABCO, which I chaired for two years. And then Trane, which was part of American Standard, was sold to Ingersoll Rand. American Standard had three major pieces of business. They did not relate very well to each other but they did hang together. They had Trane, which was their major business and a good one. They had specialty brakes, electronic brakes, anti-tilt-over devices for trucks, and various other types of gauges mainly oriented to safety. It was a smaller company with a higher margin. Then they had bath and kitchen, which most people associate with American Standard. It was one of the weakest companies, with low profit, but American Standard is a great old name and amazingly, they had a higher share of ceramic bathroom fixtures and faucets in Europe than they did in the United States. Of course, you now have Kohler here and Kohler is pretty tough.

WABCO is an interesting company because 80 percent of its operation was in eastern Europe. The other 20 percent was divided equally between the United States and Asia. But those numbers changed rapidly because Asia was picking up and the recession in Europe was tougher than here in the US. So we had this company that, at that time, did about $2.5 billion revenue as part of American Standard. We thought we could give more value to the shareholders by spinning it out. When we did, a shareholder received one share of WABCO stock for every three shares of American Standard.

It was a tax-free spin-out. WABCO started out as the old Westinghouse Air Brake Company, the originators of the air brake. At one time they had an operation in Lexington. It was an old company but the air brake had become obsolete as electronic brakes took over and became mandatory for trucks in Europe.

As I reached the American Standard Board's age limit of seventy-two, they extended my board service for an additional year. Their decision was based on all we were going through and the decisions about what to do with these pieces of the company. The board then asked me to chair WABCO because their forty-six-year-old CEO was a Frenchman who, while he had had some exposure to the United States, did not have experience with corporate governance. So we agreed that I would serve as chair for two years and then we would decide what to do. After two years we made the Frenchman chair and I served as lead director. I really enjoyed my time with WABCO. It is a worldwide company and I had regularly scheduled talks with the chairman every two weeks. I had my agenda items and he had his. I ran the board meetings.

I tried to not be on a board that included someone I knew from another board. That did not work very well. Ed Hagenlocker, a great board member for Air Products, was brought into the American Standard Board when I was on the nominating committee. But generally I tried to find places where I did not know anyone. I usually went through recruiters because I tried to find out about the company before I got too far involved in the process. It is like anything else in that when somebody asks you there is a tendency to give in and say yes. So I tried not to look at a company if I did not think I would want to be on the board. So I knew no one on most of the boards before I joined.

I operate in a rather quiet, low-key fashion. I suspect some of the boards were caught off guard by how I immersed myself in the work of the board and was always ready to give my opinions. I know I was pretty quiet when I first went on the Fleet Bank Board. That was the third board on which I served. When I went on CART, I was the only non–racecar owner on the board. At the IPO, that is the way they set it. When they put the stock on the New York Stock Exchange, it was listed with seven racecar owners and one independent. Another independent was added to the board after the first year. Fortunately, I never wanted to own a racecar.

Serving on the Lexmark Board was a new experience for me and it quickly became my most difficult board service. The situation changed over time, but when I first went on the Lexmark Board it still had several former IBM executives as members, like Frank Cary, who had been CEO of IBM. Also, one of the original people from Microsoft served on the board. I had little technical expertise so that was difficult to overcome. It reminded me of when I first went on the UK Board of Trustees. The board members sat at a table but people also sat lining the walls of the room.

I felt for a long time that I was one of the people sitting along the wall. I still like to remind my UK friends about that every so often.

I am flattered that in describing my board service people have used words and phrases such as *integrity, intelligence, insistence on simplicity where possible,* and *good humor.* But most often mentioned is my pragmatism. Somewhere along the line I became very comfortable with looking at longer-range ideas that had not been previously considered. I was sometimes alone in my position and I tended to push my ideas vigorously. I really never knew how that was coming across until afterwards when people said those nice things about me.

American Standard had a final dinner for their board but I had left the board six months earlier and did not attend. They compiled two books with comments from my colleagues along with photographs to give me. I was truly amazed at how much their comments demonstrated that they had actually been listening to me. For example, I might speak about a topic and then three months later it would happen. Often I had already forgotten about the comment I made, so it was really good to know I had made a difference.

I have always tried to take what I had learned forward with me and that came up in the comments from my American Standard colleagues. They recalled the many times during a board discussion that Jim Hardymon would say, "Well, over at Lexmark . . ." It was public information but not everybody follows Lexmark every day so I would share with them, "Over at Lexmark we did it this way." I believe I became a good board member because I had the advantage of many years of high-level experience with very good companies. I was also confident in what I recommended and advocated for. One has to reach a comfort level to be able to do that, despite occasionally getting knocked down. It sometimes takes time to reach that level of comfort.

My experience as a member of the Circuit City Board was rather sad. I suppose anyone involved in their ultimate failure could consider it a black mark on their resume. John Snow asked me to go on the Circuit City Board at a time when they were trying to strengthen the board. John Snow then became secretary of the treasury in the George W. Bush administration and left the board. The board was considered rather weak and they had a very strong CEO, Philip J. Schoonover. There were three Harvard professors on the board who were considered retail experts.

When I went on the board we were funding CarMax, a used car business, and probably not spending enough money on Circuit City stores. In turn, CarMax became a very big success. When we took CarMax out of Circuit City we lost two or three good board members who went with it. However, I think the biggest problem with Circuit City was just too many stores and too many competitors. When Walmart and Costco got into consumer electronics in a big way, Circuit City just tilted over.

People ask me why Best Buy survived and seems to be doing well while Circuit City failed. It is a good question because when I first went on the Circuit City Board, Best Buy was the company considered most likely to fail. I think once Circuit City got a little bit impregnated with CarMax they either had to go all in with CarMax or it would fail. I think we had Best Buy on the ropes when we took our foot off the accelerator and put it over onto CarMax. That is what enabled Best Buy to survive.

I served on the Fleet Bank Board with Tom Ryan, who was head of the CVS drug chain. When Best Buy hired Brad Anderson as CEO, Ryan told me, "You're going to get a pretty good competitor. That guy knows what he's doing." Turned out Ryan was right. Circuit City had 350 good stores and 250 not so good stores. If the market had allowed us to sell the 350 good stores we probably could have gotten out in good shape. But we went under before that could be done.

One of the buyers was smart enough to put a deal together to buy the 350 good stores. They were not a public company then and they would have closed the others. But the value they put on this thing was strictly on the 350, and they could not get the money. So if we had gone into bankruptcy and could have gotten the money to close the 250, we could have survived. If they had bought it either out of bankruptcy or before it went in and just operated the 350, it would still have survived as Circuit City. We were on our way out when we went into bankruptcy and we could not get any money during bankruptcy, unlike General Motors, who received help from the federal government. They went bankrupt but received an infusion of cash so they could do the things that needed to be done. They did not have to worry about digging out the cash. Circuit City did.

Another thing that really hurt us was the Circuit City website. We had a great website that worked really well and became very profitable. Since it did not have the overhead of the in-store operation, they kept lowering the prices on the website. Then somebody would go into one of the stores and say, "Hey, you got it at this price on the website," and we would have to give it to them at that price—plus still pay the person working in the store.

The Circuit City Board held thirty-five meetings in 2008 and all but about six were phone meetings. But we just could not get out of trouble even with the greatest advisors one could get. We simply ran out of money and could not borrow any. I was very disappointed in that experience. My bankruptcy attorney friends like to tell me, "You have more experience in that field than any of us. The next time we have a company in financial trouble, we are going to get you on the board." They say this tongue in cheek, I hope, but I did learn a lot about bankruptcy, perhaps too much.

As a corporate executive, I participated in three or four interesting sessions that required me to think more introspectively and evaluate myself. In the late 1960s and early 1970s it became very popular to send company people with perceived potential to sensitivity workshops or seminars. I recall one seminar in Annapolis, Maryland, that lasted an entire week. During one session we broke out into small groups and each group was given a controversial subject. The group had to report back after thirty minutes with a consensus opinion about how to deal with the subject.

For some reason, my group decided to make me chair. I

do not remember the actual subject, but after we had discussed it for several minutes, one member of our group wanted to go ahead and make a decision. Several other group members were not ready to commit and this caused some controversy within the group. But as chair of the group, I knew we had to come up with a consensus position. As we quickly approached the last ten minutes of the allotted time, I walked over to a corner of the room by myself and wrote out a position for our group. As time expired, the group had no choice but to support my draft because they had nothing else to offer.

During another session later in the week, I was required to stand at an easel in the front of the room with my back to the rest of the group and write down the comments they said about me. I still remember some of the comments, such as "sells with humor" and "chain of command oriented." Fortunately, of the thirty or forty comments coming from the audience about me, only three or four were really negative.

Those types of experiences left quite an impression on me, but I must not have learned all that I should have. I remember working around Chuck Knight during my early years at Emerson. Even though I worked with him for seventeen years, I did not report directly to him until my last six years at Emerson. I seemed to always be working on some project in which he was very interested. As stated before, he would have me in his office and say things like, "You know, there's a couple of things you should think about. If we have a list of ten items to cover and you get turned down on item seven, you are not worth a damn on items eight, nine, and ten. You also are in such a hurry to move through to the next problem or idea that sometimes you make a decision that needs a little more analysis." I will never forget his two observations about me, and I have since shared them a hundred times with other people.

I always took very seriously Chuck's suggestions regarding how I might improve my performance, even though the majority of his comments were very positive. I made one recommended change pretty quickly. I steeled myself to not let down after I had gone through an item regarding which I thought Chuck had made the wrong decision. But the second recommendation Chuck made never changed me. A person once wrote, "Hardymon thrives in the midst of complex situations that have as their hallmark the need for massive and detailed systematic change." I believe that aspect of my work personality always helped me more than it hurt.

I enjoyed interviewing prospective hires for management positions and I also liked writing the hiring agreements. Whenever someone I hired did not quite work out, Gay usually accused me of not being very good at interviewing. My procedures for evaluating management came directly from my previous experiences and how others had taught me to do it. I did not create the procedures and I have never thought of myself as being particularly creative. I bring forward ideas and practices from my experience and try to use them in places where others have not had that experience. But in a way, that itself is somewhat of a creative approach. I like process and I always believed if we had a process and adhered to it, we would achieve our goals at the end. Other people need to know where you are coming from. We may damage the process on the way through, or maybe damage each other, but if we stick to the idea that this is how we do things, everything will work out. That approach may not always work for others, but it always worked for me.

I welcomed the opportunity to speak to students at business schools about my experiences and philosophy. I began doing that at Washington University in St. Louis, where I spoke annually to an MBA class. Later, I spoke at the University of Rhode Island, Duke University, and Cornell University. I enjoyed speaking at the schools and I liked the process at Cornell the best. The Cornell students were given information regarding the background of a particular acquisition that had been completed, usually two or three years earlier. Then I would go in and discuss whether that was a good acquisition or not. I found that the students had done their preparation and they were ready for me.

The number of boards on which I served was probably greater than what most people my age would have wanted to do. In retrospect, I probably went on too many boards too quickly. I served on eleven boards, including the New York Stock Exchange public company boards, and they all provided me with rewarding experiences. The highlight of my board service was receiving the Outstanding Directors Exchange (ODX) and the Columbia Business School's Outstanding Director Award in 2005 in New York City.

Large corporations depend heavily on people who have been a CEO at another company before they hire them as CEO. Most often they come from a smaller company. That always intrigued me because, at first glance, it would not seem to be a good way to operate. But large corporations also depend on adding board members who have served on other boards because there is a learning curve upon joining a board. In fact, at JP Morgan, Jamie Dimon held an annual seminar for people who served on small company boards but aspired to be on major boards. Dimon would call on people like me who had board experience to participate in panel discussions during his seminars.

One of the most important attributes of a good board member is maintaining confidentiality. One must not talk outside the board room about what has transpired. When a new Fed chair is appointed, the media and others like to speculate on what the appointment will mean for Wall Street. Well, you do not push Wall Street out of its tracks very easily, and I am comfortable with that. Recently, there has been a lot of discussion about how the media goes about its business. If the media attempts to look into the operation of a corporation, the corporate officials can choose not to talk. You could not do that with Wall Street. If Wall Street wanted to talk about some problem they had uncovered, or you had communicated your earnings or lack of earnings or something, they would drag you through it. I am certain they are doing the same thing today.

More and more people are owning stock. Actually, some people do not even realize that they own stock because they own stocks in their various pension funds and retirement accounts. They may not even know the name of the stocks, let alone follow them very closely. But if a person has a pension they are by law told annually how well the pension fund is operating. It is an important part of our economy.

I am probably overly fond of the stock market. However, I do not get worked up over the daily ups and downs in the market. I have my own beliefs about investing and I have no desire to pick the individual stocks. That is done for me by Bessemer Trust in New York and by Bank of America in St. Louis. At one time, I had as many as five different groups investing for me. Now I have consolidated down to only two investment groups. What I like about both of them is they have large research departments. I could not expect to match the research they do when they have literally scores of people following the market closely and creating detailed records regarding how the market has done over time. All I have to do is tell them the level of risk I am willing to take.

I am a big believer in diversification. Bessemer representatives meet with me twice a year to review my level of diversification. Occasionally, they recommend changes like moving a few percentage points out of one concern and putting it into something else. I have great confidence in these types of firms. Today the investment business is a worldwide operation. There are some funds created by a country, and so I have investments in Singapore, Japan, and South Korea, to name a few. I only know it is a fund and do not know in which of their companies I am invested. Bessemer and Bank of America, of course, know the specifics of those investments, but in my report I do not get that amount of detail. Of course, I could request it, but it would not make any sense because I would not know if those companies were manufacturing, service, or made their earnings in some other way.

It seems that corporations are increasingly having to deal with political issues that can impact their profits and their stock prices. I was playing golf a few years ago with a friend who owns a large business with a nationwide market. After one of the tragic school shootings, his company was asked to lower their flag at company headquarters to half mast in support of the students. He received the request by phone while we were on the golf course.

My friend had to make a quick decision and I think he handled it better than I may have. He immediately thought, "Where does this go and where does it end? Next week it could be one of our customers who has been badly injured. Or it could go from something relatively small to a terrible tragedy or something that is especially meaningful to the people affected." That is the type of scenario that one has to be very cautious about. So my golfing friend decided right there on the fairway not to lower the flag in this instance. Generally, a corporate head benefits from having good people around him or her to consult before making statements or taking positions regarding these types of issues.

Fortunately, in the corporate world, outside social and cultural events that impact the corporation are the exception and not the rule. Generally, one does not have a reporter running up to you and sticking a microphone in your face. It is not that type of life. For issues we anticipated would be sensitive, we did simulations or run-throughs about how we would handle those issues. A group of people would get with me and grill me on how I would respond to certain situations and try to anticipate questions.

My financial package from Textron gave me the capability to explore experiences that others perhaps could not. For example, I have always been very interested in sports. Gayle Sayers, the great player for the Chicago Bears, worked for us at SKIL in Chicago, making it easy to be very involved with the Chicago sports scene. I became interested in IndyCar racing because of my association with racecar drivers Bobby Rahal and Roberto Guerrero. I eventually served on the board of Championship Auto Racing Teams, known at CART.

I also became involved in the horse business on a small scale when I invested in some Thoroughbred stallions and attended periodic meetings with the other investors. Under the name of Dogwood Stables, Cot Campbell established an arrangement for group ownership that had never been done before. There had been previous efforts to get partnerships of owners together, like had been done with Funny Cide. Other times business partners might go together to own a horse. In our arrangement, Campbell brought together investors who did not even know one another. The shareholders had no maintenance obligations. Shareholders only had to add their name and put their money at risk. Suddenly, one of the five horses we "owned" began winning races as a two-year-old.

I bought a second year of five yearlings and then a third year. Out of that first group came Summer Squall, who finished second to Unbridled in the 1990 Kentucky Derby and then won the Preakness. I attended the Preakness that year and I must admit it was very exciting. During that last quarter of a mile, Gay said I was hollering so loud that everybody around us was looking at me.

When I joined the University of Kentucky Board of Trustees, Robert Clay also served on the board. I had gotten to know him a little bit during my tenure on the board, but I knew him much better afterwards. Before long he approached me about investing in a stallion fund. I think one other time before I had gone back and done some investing with Cot Campbell, but that time it was not successful. But then I got back in the horse business at Robert Clay's urging. My involvement with horse racing was very minor, but it was fun while it lasted.

I am sometimes asked my opinion about executive compensation being tied to the company stock. I think that executives or board members should be tied to the shareholder, and stock options are a pretty good way to do that. Now, sometimes this arrangement gets out of hand because they start fixing the books to make the stocks look better. It is just too attractive to have something sitting there at $30 a share if I could buy it for $20 a share and sell it for $30. That becomes real money. So executive stock options have gotten somewhat of a bad name because of that occasionally happening.

During times when the stock market performed more erratically, either up or down, the trend has been towards restricted stock. Restricted stock means rights to shares of stock based on some incentive plan and you have to accomplish that incentive. If you accomplish the incentive and the stock goes up, you will obviously make money. If you do not accomplish the incentive, you do not receive more money. If you halfway do it, the stock may not have gone up as much as you like, but you will get something. With stock options you could very well have them underwater, which means the value at the time of exercise of the option is less than at the time of the grant. During the Great Recession most of the boards I served on had their shares underwater. It took a while but I suspect most have recovered their value.

The last recession, more commonly referred to as the Great Recession, was really tough on businesses. I hoped at the time that businesses would come out of it feeling very strong and start growing again. Business leaders sometimes need reminding that recessions occur when things get out of balance. The best manager in the world could not have taken a company through the Great Recession without it being affected. I worry that it might make people begin asking, "What is the use of fourteen family moves and twelve-hour days when somebody is going to wipe everything out around the corner?"

Views about work have changed during my lifetime. There seems to be more focus on quality of life issues, or at least more talk about it. I hope we do not change to the extent that an entrepreneur does not stop creating small businesses just because one day down the line he might have to bankrupt them. Or that the college MBA student does not jump into a company at the lower end and strive to work their way up just because they think there will be a real recession at some point. The Great Recession, the worse economic downturn since the Great Depression, seemed to have made a strong impression on the financial community.

But most impressions do not last, and as the years passed the impressions I came away with from the 1982–1983 downturn grew weaker and weaker over time. All I know now is that we survived and did well shortly afterwards.

I often think about my grandfather out on the farm. My grandparents had rugs in every room and when we would go out there to spend the night I would sometimes pull back a rug to find cash under it. As a child I thought it was just the weirdest thing I had ever seen. Of course, I came to understand later that he had lived through a time when if you had all your cash in a bank you could very easily lose it. He had not quite caught up to the fact that the country now had federal deposit insurance.

Most agree that the twentieth century was the American century, but some wonder if the twenty-first century will be the Chinese century. I was on six boards for investment firms. One of their smaller companies did $300 million in sales, another did about $2 billion, and the others were somewhere in between. Of the six companies only two actually manufacture product. The others are like Lexmark in that they do not make anything. They only develop the software and then the complete unit is made by a contractor. Another one of the companies is a distributor of automobile and truck tires while another is a distributor of truck parts for class 1 trucks. Still another company is a distributor of packaging like shampoo bottles and similar items, but they do not make them. They develop the design and contract with a supplier.

WABCO does make product, but none of the manufacturing is based in the United States. I think our position relative to the Chinese will eventually level off to where they are going to have to spend more money as we do in this country to satisfy their workers. I do not know if they want to think about healthcare for their citizens and how people live, but they may need to eventually improve on both.

We work with many other really economically depressed countries like those in South America and elsewhere. They do not produce much and therefore pose no economic threat to the US.

However, China is a serious competitor. I remember when Ireland was the place one bought stuff from or when Belgium was a supply center. All these things change over time and I think that China will change as well.

The question is, when will somebody venture out and start building something like farm equipment in the United States again? I do not know, but right now we are researching and developing new products in this country and getting them made elsewhere. The day is going to come when we see that we can make new products here again. Then things will begin to level out a bit. I am predicting that something will likely happen by the middle of this century. I can make these statements but I will not be here to defend them. I am really not sure how quickly the changes will happen.

The United States has become much more competitive since the last Great Recession. We have cut out a lot of overhead, but we could easily lose that edge if we have to supply the money to run the government out of a smaller base of fewer workers, less property tax collected because the recession highlighted too many houses, too many bad loans, and too many electronic stores. But one thing we can always count on is change. Ted Turner left a big impression on me when he wrote in his book, *Call Me Ted,* that there were 2 billion people in this world when he was born and there will be 8 billion when his lifespan ends. That changes a lot of things.

Another good example from my board service is that boards now tend to talk more about compensation programs than they do about where a particular product is made. They don't even know where the product is made. So that is another big change. Back in the 1980s we moved manufacturing from New England to the southern states. We moved forty plants in the 1980s and early 1990s during that recession. Moving our manufacturing operations was a large part of my job during that time. But most of the relocated plants stayed in the United States, other than the twelve plants that went to Mexico. That was only thirty or thirty-five years ago.

I still enjoy continuing to do some work even in retirement more than I thought I would. Having gained all of this experience, it is nice to continue using it for a purpose. While climbing up the career ladder I constantly looked for ways to advance. Well, now I am going nowhere and I am not looking for anything. It either comes to me or it does not happen which, after all those years in business, is a most interesting feeling. I would not want to have had this freedom to do nothing when I was twenty-five or I would have become a bum. But this stage of my life is very satisfying. I only regret that the years now pass by so rapidly. But of course that is the cycle of life. I like to plan ahead so I know what I am going to do the following week and the week after that. I am afraid that approach also has a way of accelerating time. But I am enjoying my life and if I did not have things to do that I found satisfying it would not be a good situation for me.

Chapter Six

Giving Back to My Alma Mater

I suppose that the university administration
and some of the board members
viewed my corporate background as something
that could be helpful to UK. It is more of a
commitment than one might think it would be.

Perhaps my most interesting and gratifying board experiences came with my appointment to the University of Kentucky Board of Trustees in 1992. I am sure UK president Charles Wethington, who I had known since he had moved to Maysville in 1971 to build and open a new community college, had considerable influence on my appointment. My initial appointment ran for only one year. Prior to my appointment, the state legislature vacated all university boards in Kentucky. A new system for board appointments was then implemented requiring a nominating committee to send names to the governor for consideration for appointment. Before that, each governor had selected whoever they wished, usually someone who had supported their political aspirations. Since all of the appointments were new, the terms had to be staggered, resulting in my initial one-year appointment. I took great pride in being the first out-of-state resident ever appointed to the UK Board. After my first year on the board, Governor Jones reappointed me to a regular six-year term, from 1993 to 1999. After being off the board for a few years I was appointed again in 2003.

The responsibilities of an executive committee of corporate

or university boards are similar. There are specific functions an executive committee has authority to handle between full board meetings. Normally, executive committees cannot make an acquisition or sell an asset. But there are procedural issues that an executive committee can deal with, and of course at the next board meeting the executive committee minutes are reviewed and then the board as a whole has the opportunity to discuss. The board's authority over an executive committee is probably narrowed down to "Don't do that again!" I am sure it varies somewhat from board to board, but if you just do not change the assets you have authority.

When I first went on the UK Board the executive committee was made up of three members. When I became chair of the finance committee I also went on the executive committee. So even though I was a new board member who had not yet met all of the other members, they knew that as finance committee chair I would be placed on the executive committee.

I did not find the transition from corporate boards to a university board very difficult. We had revenues and expenses and a balance sheet showing cash and other assets and liabilities. One difference was that the university did not have accrual accounting, which I used in my corporate work. In fact, the use of accrual accounting by corporations started being overdone. As a corporate leader, when my company had a good quarter and we found ourselves somewhat ahead of what we had told Wall Street, I could establish a reserve fund for things like future restructuring, with no time limits on use of the fund. Corporations are no longer allowed to operate that way but are required to print the earnings they make each quarter at the end of that quarter.

The university was very different because essentially it was ahead of the game. You could not carry much over from one fiscal year to another without a good reason. Slowly, that has changed to some degree whereby more leeway is allowed, as with the hospital, for example. With the hospital we were able to hold onto some things, particularly cash, because a hospital periodically has such big expenditures, such as purchasing a piece of equipment for millions of dollars. It was not possible to make that type of purchase within one quarter. We made those changes and I had no trouble with that.

The thing I found most difficult with the finance committee was that many different items like patents came before us that had nothing to do with finance. I never knew what was going to come through the finance committee. During the early days I chaired the committee I would meet with President Wethington and board chairman Edward T. "Ned" Breathitt to review some items before I took them to the committee so that I could better understand what I was getting into. Some of that has changed as the committee system has expanded.

I felt some pressure to make sure I attended every board meeting. I had asked my Textron Board if I should accept the UK Board appointment because I tried never to miss a scheduled meeting. I decided that if I was going to take this on I needed to look ahead on my calendar to determine any conflicts. If there were conflicts on the days the board met, I would not take that assignment or I would rearrange my schedule. I traveled extensively anyway, so I was always coming from somewhere or going to somewhere. I simply made one of my stops Kentucky. The one-year appointment did not bother me because it gave me the opportunity to see if serving on the UK Board would work for me considering my other obligations. It never entered my mind that I should have had a longer appointment.

I had been friends with President Wethington for many years and suddenly I was serving on the board for which he worked. I did not find that arrangement awkward, but other members of the board sometimes raised the issue with me. It might have been awkward if I had not been qualified to serve on the board, but I knew I was.

Over the years President Wethington had talked about the university and his work. Most things one needs to know about the university are public information, but a board member obviously gets into greater depth on a multitude of issues. President Wethington knew my career and what I had done. We remained pretty independent of each other. We went different ways in our lives and I never found that to be much of a problem. I did not even know Governor Jones, who had appointed me, nor did I ever have any political ties in Kentucky. I was not beholden to anyone.

During that first year on the board the local media had little influence on me. I did not subscribe to the Lexington or Louisville newspapers because I did not live in Kentucky, and this was before one could read the papers online. I always took the Maysville paper because my mother still lived there and I wanted to keep up with what was going on in my hometown. But one would not find anything negative about UK in the Maysville paper. Later, when I lived in Kentucky and served as board chair, the first thing I did every morning was read the local paper to check for any news or commentary about UK.

Adequate state support has historically been an issue for UK. I believe that when I first joined the UK board, roughly 45 percent of the university's budget came from state dollars. UK's total budget was smaller than it is now but when state funds decreased 4 or 5 percent it was significant. Some board members and the president may have spoken to the governor or some legislators about it, but most of us had very little control. I did find that very difficult.

I believe a university like UK would be better off if it could have a sufficient endowment to become independent from the state. In that scenario the state could continue assisting with particular projects and programs rather than the university being so dependent on the state's general fund. That is where the trouble lies. You can always delay a particular project and wait until the economy picks back up. But general fund dollars are essential to the university's undergraduate program, which is the foundation of the entire operation. For other operations such as food services and housing, just to name two, the university continues to look for more efficiency and creative ways to manage nonacademic units.

UK athletics does not receive any state dollars and is self-supporting. I can envision a time when the Gatton College of Business and Economics and the UK College of Law might become self-supporting as well. Of the university's professional schools, the College of Engineering would probably have a more difficult time making that transition. But by making at least some of the colleges self-supporting, the rest of the monies that come from the state's general fund could be allocated for arts and sciences and colleges that cannot make it on private support alone.

For many years UK faced major challenges in maintaining and building new facilities. Because of an insufficient K-12 education system and the pressure on UK to increase its number of graduates, the university needed more students to live on campus and learn in smaller classrooms so that they could receive more individual instruction. So in the past decade, UK has used creative financing to build additional living/learning spaces for students and has employed private gifts to renovate academic buildings or build new ones. It is impossible to continue increasing the number of students and faculty unless there are sufficient resources to support those students and faculty.

I made a gift to support an endowed chair in urology and Dr. Natasha Kyrpianou was recruited for the position. I was amazed and saddened to learn that they put her desk in a hallway due to a lack of space. The same was true when UK recruited Dr. Mark Evers and his high-powered team of cancer researchers. Fortunately, space became available in the new Lee T. Todd Pharmacy Building. But additional space for information technologies in the campus's Digital Village and similar areas continues to be a pressing need if UK is to recruit the type of students and faculty needed for Kentucky's flagship research university.

Planning for what would become the William T. Young Library was well under way when I joined the board. We were still involved in property acquisition for the library even as legislative support was first promised and then taken away. Planning for the new library began with a legislative endorsement, with a clear indication that funding would come later. When the members of the legislature changed their minds regarding funding it did not affect me as much as others.

My mentor Chuck Knight was a great long-range thinker. Occasionally, I would meet with him and he would start into something that, if it was not 180 degrees off from where he was previously on the subject, it was at least 90 degrees. I would say, "Chuck, remember when you said such and such?" He'd reply, "I said that at that time. This is now and we have to deal with the way it is now." He always reserved the right to change his mind. But his logic for changing his position usually made sense. So when the legislature decided not to fund the library after a previous legislature had indicated it would, I was not surprised. But I was just as committed as everybody else regarding how we were going to move forward with the project.

One should never overlook the great job President Wethington did with the project to construct a new main library for UK. But the support of William T. Young and his ability to obtain the support of other private donors made the project possible. In addition to giving his own money, Bill Young came to us with a portfolio of people he intended to tap for support. Moreover, Charles and Bill together never let us think that we should delay or give up on the library project. Leaders are there to guide us through dark times, and Charles led us through this one.

As events unfolded, I thought we would have to scale the library plans back some because that is the way I always approach projects. That wish list is normally something you can work on a little bit as you go through a project. By that time in my career, I had seen too many people bringing projects to me and presenting the numbers in an overly optimistic manner just so they would have room to cut back later. But that was not the way Bill Young operated because he never compromised. He operated the same way a few years later when I served on the Transylvania University Board with him. Once Bill decided he was going to do something a certain way, that is how it would be done. Fortunately, the William T. Young Library has been a great success.

I served a three-year term as chair of the board from 2006 to 2008. I could have served one more year as chair but chose not to. I was followed as chair by UK's first and to date only woman board chair, Myra Ball. The role of board chair primarily entails running the board meetings and being involved in the work of the university. However, I have been more involved with UK since Eli Capilouto became president than I ever was as the board chair. President Capilouto has a knack of utilizing me where he thinks my talents are most needed. The many strategic initiatives he has made have aligned more with my strengths.

Not everybody wants to serve as board chair of the UK Board, and if they do, most choose not to serve very long. When I became chair, the board chose that year not to elevate the vice chair, Jo-Etta Wickliffe. I do not remember a lot about the controversy or at least it was not discussed much. One of the small differences between a university board and the corporate boards I served on was that between board meetings I seldom saw or interacted with other members of the board because they were scattered across the state and everyone was involved in very different things. Perhaps there was more of an undercurrent going on among the UK Board than I realized because I lived outside Kentucky. I did not have a clique of people that I chatted with about the board between meetings.

I suppose that the university administration and some of the board members viewed my corporate background as something that could be helpful to UK. As chair, I ran the meetings like I would have run a corporate board meeting and tried to keep the board on track. I was not interested in having somebody drop a topic that was not on the original agenda into the meeting completely out of the blue. I recall a couple of times some people in the audience tried to speak up, but I tried to control those things.

I think most of the board members agreed with my approach to running the meetings.

One issue that became controversial while I served on the board in 2004 was the renovation of the Hilary J. Boone Center, which had opened as a "faculty club" towards the end of President Otis Singletary's administration. When UK president Lee Todd decided to renovate the Boone Center, the *Lexington Herald-Leader* criticized the $4.4 million renovation plan as unwise during an economic downturn. At the time, I chaired the board's finance committee and was quoted in the newspaper saying, "'There was more to look at than I first realized. We need a full explanation of this." I wanted to find out how the project got approval from the legislative oversight committee before it was presented for approval by the UK Board. I noted at the time that we had not been able to determine how that happened.

The Boone Center renovation project became very controversial mostly because of the way it was managed. President Todd's and his wife Patsy's very close involvement with the project, combined with its overall cost, worried me some at the time. In spite of the controversy, the renovated Boone Center has proven to be a real winner. The center improved the quality of its menu and it became more heavily used, resulting in a better financial outlook. But I must say, at the time I was more than a little leery about the project and put a slowdown on it until the details of the project became clearer.

Another issue that arose during my time on the board was the evaluation of the president and the use of a bonus to reward him for meeting targeted goals for the university. I felt very strongly that we should try to implement a review process for the president and I said at the time that I did not know how long the process might last. But I truly believed it was something that needed to be done. It did not take long for the media to focus on what score the president received. One year President Todd received a score of 92 and the media questioned whether that indicated the president was not doing well. I remember telling the press, "Well, you know, that's a pretty good grade." We cited the successes of President Todd in areas like bettering the quality of the incoming freshmen as well as increasing the university's endowment and outside research funding.

In the corporate world I had been used to offering bonuses to executives for good performances. UK had given bonuses previously, but they were not based on any type of evaluation score or grade. I wanted to get to a situation where it was easier to explain why we chose to award a bonus and what percentage of the total possible bonus would be given. That had worked well for me in my corporate experiences with both Emerson and Textron.

I also wanted some way to control the penalties we were getting from the National Collegiate Athletic Association (NCAA). I believe that UK had been penalized every decade since the 1940s. During my freshman year at UK the basketball team was banned from playing that season. So the first criterion of the bonus for President Todd included a 10 percent bonus depending on whether or not we received any penalties for a major NCAA violation. That was a little unusual because normally the blame for infractions is placed on the athletic department and the coaches. The president generally escaped blame or accountability. As it turned out, we did not have any NCAA violations between 2000 and 2010. So at least we put an end to the previous record of one violation every decade.

In 2005 the board voted to construct a new UK hospital. I said at the time, "This will likely be this board's most important decision." I still agree with that assessment. In addition, acquiring Good Samaritan Hospital was a really important step in building the new hospital. Good Samaritan was only 40 percent utilized and in rather dire financial straits. UK Healthcare utilized this vacant space and was able to keep growing during the construction of the new hospital. Moreover, it was prime property adjacent to the university that could eventually be used for other purposes.

During the planning and actual construction of the new hospital there were several changes made. The first increased the size of the new parking garage being built across Limestone from the new hospital. In addition, we added an additional floor to the hospital. But we stayed within our budget and construction remained on schedule. I became a strong supporter of the construction company for the hospital and was very glad they also constructed the new residence halls. Building the new hospital was the right thing to do at the right time and Michael Karpf, UK's executive vice president for health affairs, was the right person to lead it.

Not long after we approved construction of a new hospital, a plan to build a new basketball practice facility came before the board. Plans called for a nearly $30 million project funded with private money and the issuance of $7 million in bonds. Because it was to be built with private funds, it was a difficult project to turn down. However, three members of the board—two faculty and one staff—voted against the project. Still, there were a lot of people interested in supporting the project, including me. I have always been impressed with UK director of athletics Mitch Barnhart's leadership. I felt confident he would do the right thing with the practice facility project, and he did.

As my term on the board ended, I took some time to reflect on what had occurred. I always did this whenever I left a corporate board. I would usually list the four or five things I was most proud to have been involved in as a board member. It was not an attempt to take personal credit. I was just happy to have been a part of certain achievements.

Number one in regard to my UK Board service was the new hospital and not only the new building, but all of the changes that occurred within UK Healthcare. I understood the strategy of the hospital more than I did any other part of the university. I think the approach of going out into the state and creating relationships with local and regional hospitals has been very successful. UK built trusted relationships with Kentucky hospitals by assuring them UK was not going to rob them of their patients. Instead, their patients could stay local until the point where they required more advanced or specialized care. Now those patients can come to UK rather than having to go to Nashville, Cincinnati, or Rochester. Kentuckians can get the care they need in Lexington.

Of course there is much more to be done and it is important to have the right people in the right place at the right time. It is almost more important than individual capability because if you put a high-growth person into a leadership position when you do not have any money to spend, you are wasting that talent. In addition, that person will ultimately become frustrated and then the management or administration will become frustrated with that person.

It might surprise some people who do not follow higher education closely how much emphasis universities now place on retaining and graduating students. When I went to college, the general approach was that you either made it or you didn't. It was considered to be your choice. College was viewed more as a filter and only a certain number were even expected to make it through that filter. Now that has completely changed because we need more educated citizens and universities need the revenue from those students who had been leaving the university.

I began to pay much more attention to retention and graduation rates when I became involved with UK's medical school. I was fascinated to learn that out of ninety-two people who came in as medical students, ninety-one graduated. In-depth interviews with the ones who did not make it found that, in most cases, they had simply decided they did not want to be physicians.

Now in Kentucky, which is not viewed as the education capital of the world, one sees a more deliberate push for a better-rounded student. I witnessed that when my granddaughter began looking at colleges. Schools have begun looking not just at grades and test scores but also at what a prospective student has done in their life in regard to other activities. I believe this is a much better approach.

There were some initiatives during my time on the board that did not work as well and that I would have handled differently if I had it to do over. One was the whole fiasco over a proposed retirement village. We jumped at a plan to place a retirement development at Coldstream Research Park, but it was not really fully thought out. Still, we decided to try it and took it to the board. As I learned more about what the chair should and should not do, I would more closely watch the agenda for some of those types of things.

Also, I do not know if the process for evaluating the president is going to survive. I thought when we instituted the process that it provided a scorecard on which to base the paying of a bonus to the president. After I left the board I think there were very few board members with experience doing that type of evaluation. And even though he came from the business world, President Lee Todd was not used to an evaluation process. He had not been in that part of the business. But I had high hopes for the evaluation process and I was interviewed by the *Chronicle of Higher Education* and even *USA Today* about what we were doing. Other universities also began contacting us to get more information about the process. So, overall I remain proud of what I contributed to the UK Board during my time there.

Following the successful library campaign, President Wethington turned a lot of his attention to conducting the university's first capital campaign. I remember the first meeting to discuss it like it was yesterday. We met in President Wethington's living room at Maxwell Place with a consultant brought in from Chicago. I do not remember everyone who was in the room, but Terry Mobley, UK's vice president for development, participated. As the discussion about a possible campaign began, it was all very new to me. I am a much better giver than solicitor of gifts. I had never really given much thought to how a university capital campaign might work. But after the meeting that night I came away with two impressions. First, to be successful we anticipated having to raise several hundred million dollars. Second, the consultant told us in no uncertain terms how poorly equipped we were to pull off a successful campaign. I remember those two things more vividly than whether I thought UK could complete a successful capital campaign. Later, when the numbers started moving up with the help of state matching funds, known as "Bucks for Brains," I became pretty sure we could reach our goal. I am very pleased I was around for the capital campaign, and of course going forward the university will conduct campaigns every few years. They have become almost normal business operation in higher education.

An important thing to keep in mind about philanthropy is that people who give are always anxious to see others give. We believe in the cause we give to and we believe that cause needs the help of others as well as our own. I assume President Wethington had a lot of assistance from his development office and from his college deans with fundraising. I know from personal experience that Dean Tom Lester in engineering was very good in the development arena and kept the concept of the Digital Village, which is important to me, moving forward. But there are areas of the university where philanthropy is not as vibrant. Perhaps that is because they do not have someone to champion their college as Bill Gatton has done for the College of Business and Economics.

One of my proudest moments came when the newspaper ran a list of the top-ten all-time donors to UK. First, just making a list like that is good. Second, I was proud I generated most of the money within my immediate family. That is a really good feeling and it does not need to be publicized too much further. I do not know where I am on the list now because I'm aware that others have made some large donations since then.

I had close ties to Kentucky's community college system because of the community college located in Maysville. And, of course, Charles Wethington was the founding director of that college. Obtaining a community college is an important step for any city or town in Kentucky, and Maysville was no exception. The college received widespread community support. The community assembled a group led by one of my two mentors, Frank Jones, which made it possible for every student in the surrounding area to at least pay their tuition and get their books. Room and board was not an issue because all of the students commuted. I was pleased to have the opportunity to support that program for my hometown, and it also attracted the support of many other people.

So when I thought about Kentucky's community colleges, I did not see them in a political sense of connecting UK to the entire state. I simply supported the concept of community colleges and would have supported the college in Maysville regardless of which university placed it there. It met an important need for our community. A small but funny example: I remember when Emerson Electric acquired Browning Manufacturing in 1968. At the time we were doing $30 million in volume. Emerson wanted to attend some presentations and somebody was smart enough to ask, "How does Emerson normally do presentations?" Apparently they used transparencies and a projector in their presentations, so we decided to use transparencies in our presentation except we did not have a projector. Fortunately, we were able to borrow one from the community college. In many more significant ways the community college impacted Maysville and still does today.

My early association with the community college convinced me that from a strictly leverage standpoint of the financials, community colleges were very important to the growth of the university. I still believe UK's main campus would be larger now if we had the community college system because we would have been able to put our dollars to better use. UK would have gotten more dollars, they would have spread them around more, and the spread probably would have affected the main campus more than it would have Maysville, Kentucky. By that I mean there would be only one president, one big library, one system, one process, one curriculum, and they could draw off UK.

During the debate over removing the community colleges from UK, I went by myself to see Governor Paul Patton. I probably had some help from UK getting the appointment; I do not remember. The governor sat behind his desk during our meeting and I said to him, "If you want UK to grow, then it has a better chance of growing with the size it has and the diversity of its current operations. You talk about keeping the assets involved year-round and there is a much better chance of doing that with the community colleges as part of UK." But of course he was the governor and he did not know me very well then. He might have listened a little better now. He did not listen that day. He simply said, "I thank you for sharing that. I disagree." He did not believe that keeping the community colleges with UK was best for reaching the state's educational goals. Perhaps he was right if one agrees with President Todd's reasoning that UK can help Kentucky more by aspiring to be a top-twenty national research university.

So then the questions might be, were the community colleges holding back UK's aspirations and was UK keeping the community colleges from being all that they could and should be? Perhaps I was not in a good position to know those answers. The Maysville Community College is still doing okay today and I continue to get requests for donations from the college. At the time of the debate there were hard positions taken on each side. I suppose some historian will come down on one side and probably another historian will come down on the other side of this issue. Some saw Patton's move as part of a larger educational reform. Others saw it as the governor trying to diminish UK's political influence across the state.

The most disappointing meeting during my thirteen years on the UK Board was the time Governor Patton came to speak to the board about the community colleges. I had been told to stop all board business upon his arrival. I remember I was giving a finance report, which was always lengthy in those days. I do not know why I remember this, perhaps it is my engineering background, but I was just finishing item number four of my report when the governor walked into the eighteenth-floor meeting room in Patterson Tower. President Wethington's wife, Judy, and daughter, Lisa, were at the meeting, perhaps because they also knew the governor was coming. Governor Patton stood at the head of the long board room table and proceeded to tear into us. It was really unbelievable. He essentially told us, "You either do it my way or you're gone." Nobody said a word, raised their hand, applauded, or booed. Then the governor left.

An uneasy silence permeated the room. Finally, I spoke up: "Item number five." I will never forget that moment. I waited a good while because I did not know if President Wethington intended to offer a rebuttal to the governor's harsh comments or if somebody else was going to speak up for the board. Everyone sat there seemingly in shock. It was especially awkward for one of the board members who had been to a meeting in Frankfort that morning and had ridden over to Lexington with the governor and walked into the meeting with him. He is still a close friend and I know he had no idea regarding the intensity of what the governor was going to do. He thought it was just a normal ride through the countryside and a chance to chat with the governor.

Since I traveled back and forth from Providence for the board meetings, I suspect I missed a lot of in-fighting going on within the board. I had no way of knowing what was being said among the board members when I was not part of those discussions. I had gone to see the governor face-to-face to tell him my position. He would not have heard my opinions from any other source.

There is no better way to influence a leader than to go to his or her board with either a positive or negative message. It makes a tremendous impact if somebody marches into the boardroom and offers a critique. I suppose the governor simply decided he was going to take his concerns right to the source.

It was a tough fight over the community colleges, and UK's attorney was very aggressive on it. He was actually a little bit hard to manage, if that is the right word. He was so intense in this it became difficult to get the help we needed from him. The proposed legislation to separate the community colleges from UK was not entirely clear regarding what it would do or what we were supposed to do. So we decided that the best thing for us to do was put our best foot forward and if somebody said, "You're going against the rules," it was up to them to tell us.

Probably an equally important issue in Kentucky higher education is the unhealthy, costly rivalry between the University of Louisville and the University of Kentucky. When the two universities compete rather than cooperate, it takes a toll on our time, our funds, and our human capacities. I believe there is room enough in Kentucky higher education for each university to have its own strategy. But whether Governor Patton meant this to happen or not, we went through a period in which his decision pulled UK down to where the space between Louisville and UK became less. I have never had another conversation with Governor Patton about the community colleges or higher education generally. But he did reappoint me to the UK Board after four years off.

The actual transition of the community colleges away from UK went pretty well. UK protected its assets to a certain extent, even keeping the community college in Lexington for a time. President Lee Todd always seemed concerned about the loss of UK's political clout and I understand why he felt that way.

If there is one takeaway from this memoir, it is never to overstay your welcome because I have never seen that work out well. As I mentioned earlier, I nearly overstayed my time at Textron. Those situations arise when you have people around you who think you cannot be quickly replaced, or are afraid that your departure is going to affect them, or simply believe that "Stay" is what you want to hear. But once the subject of leaving comes up, you are starting down the slide. Now, as I sit on boards at my age, once the board starts discussing change or the CEO tells the board that he is thinking of a transition, you know the slide has begun.

The controversial vote on President Wethington's contract extension occurred at my last board meeting in June 1999. I assume the more politically astute board members knew that they would be losing a vote for President Wethington when I left the board. I do not remember who else went off the board at that time, but for whatever reason, I knew I was not going to be reappointed. Maybe it was because I had not been asked to send in an application. They did things differently then, but I knew I was going off the board.

I still have the document about the president's contract. I saw it the other day when I was looking through some of my papers. I do not even know if it is public information, but we had a document. I came to the meeting knowing there would be few who would challenge it. But I had so much confidence in Governor Breathitt, who served as board chair at the time, and so much confidence in President Wethington's grasp of things that I was almost certain that the two of them thought they had the votes for the contract extension.

So we went into the room for lunch, and towards the end of the lunch meeting Breathitt went through all the rigmarole to move the board into a closed session to discuss a personnel issue. Perhaps the pre-selling had not been good enough. For instance, it is very hard to go into a meeting like that and have a document thrown out that people had not yet seen. Maybe the reason it was not shown was because they expected trouble. I never asked. Governor Breathitt, with whom I had become fairly close since we had started playing golf together, explained the document and everybody just kind of nodded and we went back into the board room. Nobody said a word. Then, as I remember, Breathitt called for a voice vote on the president's contract extension. The yea and nay vote was so uncertain that we went around the table and voted individually. The vote ended up in a tie, which meant it did not pass.

I am still not sure what happened—and again, nobody said anything. I had attended the board meetings but I was not involved in any of the backroom conversations. At that time I was making trips to the Lahey Clinic in Boston for my cancer treatments and Gay and I were trying to get ourselves established in Florida. I had learned that I had prostate cancer so I was kind of slow getting involved in the Lexington community. This was before the operation but I already knew I was going to have the surgery.

It was a troubling time and probably illustrates why I do not belong in an open records society. In the corporate world, when it came to really controversial issues, I spent time talking with my board. I would call the members individually and talk with them, trying to give them the data I thought they needed to make an informed decision. The Textron Board turned me down only once on a major acquisition. It was early in my tenure as CEO and I never let that happen again. But I'm thankful it did happen that time because not moving ahead with the acquisition I proposed left us with enough money to buy Cessna, which proved to be a tremendously positive acquisition.

I think UK is in a better position now than I have ever seen it. That is no reflection on all the university's previous achievements over the years. The university is slowly evolving into an operation more like what I was used to in the business world. Of course, I suspect that makes most faculty suspicious. But I had to be somewhat careful in my relationship with UK because occasionally I would become frustrated. It seems to me that UK is now getting better students and the retention and graduation rates continues to improve. Various areas within UK are also getting ranked higher nationally.

In recent years I believe that UK has spent its facilities money wisely. I have enjoyed working closely with President Capilouto on some really interesting projects. I had no involvement with the search that hired Capilouto but I did get a lot of good feedback from people like Bill Gatton who went to Birmingham to see what was going on and check Capilouto out. I felt comfortable with President Capilouto's selection even though I did not know him. I had been off the board quite a while before he arrived.

Apparently President Capilouto learned about my background and my work with UK Healthcare, especially in regard to the construction of the new hospital. In 2012 he contacted me and asked me to consider serving on a committee to look at outside funding for new residence halls. He suggested that the first thing we should do was visit the current residence halls on campus. So I and a few others spent part of a Thanksgiving weekend going through the mostly empty residence halls evaluating their condition and livability.

I really had no idea the dormitories were in such bad shape. When my granddaughter attended UK, she lived in one of the newer buildings that had been constructed during the Todd administration. I had visited those new buildings but not the older ones, some of which were built before I was a UK student. The low ceilings in the two high-rise towers first caught my attention. I supposed they were constructed that way to cut costs. It was claustrophobic even for a little guy like me.

I was the only person on the dormitory committee who was "retired," so I had the time to work on the project. I worked with UK staff to prepare and issue a request for proposals. President Capilouto knew about a new dormitory at the University of Alabama that was funded by a group that made a proposal to us. But we got a slew of responses. Some of them were just entrepreneurs and you could not tell whether they had or could secure the financial capacity to do a project like ours. We had to sort all of that out working with Bob Wiseman, UK's vice president for facilities, and the UK Purchasing Department. Wiseman was very helpful throughout the entire process, as was Mark Kornbluh, the dean of arts and sciences, and Merle Hackbart, the interim dean of the Gatton College. As we got further into the project, I could sense the university administrators looking to me more. Perhaps they thought I might go running to the president if one of them did something that did not have my support. Eventually I gained their confidence and they became more candid in our conversations.

Ultimately, we brought in three groups. The largest, American Campus, was an outfit from New York. The second was EdR from Memphis, and the third was a group that had done the residence hall at Alabama. So I went to the New York Stock Exchange and through one of the people who invests for me, I got pretty good reports on these people and their capabilities.

It turned out that, in my opinion, all three were qualified. So each came to campus and made a presentation. Frankly, Randy

Churchey and his EdR group made the best presentation. I had been around big business in New York long enough to know that American Campus would be difficult to deal with; they began negotiating almost from the time they made their presentation. I was not sure how we would handle that because, just based on the numbers, they were the biggest and had the most experience. But I just knew we would have difficult negotiations with them. By the end of the process we all got on the same page: the recommendation was unanimous for EdR. I suppose my experience and the information I gathered and shared with the group helped. It would have been more difficult for the committee to make a recommendation if they had not had somebody accumulating the necessary background information. The committee members proved to be good readers and good analysts. After we selected EdR, we held a meeting on campus with EdR and also brought in several analysts from New York. During that meeting one of the analysts told the group I was responsible for EdR getting the job. President Capilouto stayed out of the entire process but was always very supportive of me. I would meet with him regularly and keep him informed. When I told him which firm the committee recommended for the project he approved it.

There were a number of fortunate circumstances regarding the residence hall project. For one thing, we built the first buildings during a downturn in the national economy. That allowed us to set up a contract that made it affordable for UK and profitable for EdR. For better or worse for the university, I knew EdR had to report to Wall Street what they were doing so we could not just squeeze everything out of them. We decided that in order to assure less controversy, we would do a separate contract for each residence hall. This had a lot to do with both the economy and student enrollment.

With Haggin Hall, the first resident built, I thought it would be best if EdR owned the buildings and we essentially leased from them. I thought the city would overlook the property tax considering the hundreds of millions of dollars we were putting into the local economy with the dormitories and the new hospital. Well, as it turned out, the city would not give on the tax so EdR continues to pay tax on that one dormitory. I take the blame for that.

Fool me once, shame on you; fool me twice, shame on me. We went for a land-lease arrangement on the other new residence halls. EdR leases the land from UK and UK receives a percentage of the revenue. We started out at 12 percent and the last residence hall was 10 percent. After EdR gets their return, we get 25 percent of the overage. We set up that formula because we did not want EdR to raise the housing price abnormally. By reviewing the number annually, one can factor in changes in the economy.

EdR got the buildings constructed on time and provided maintenance. They put in a marketing department to help fill those buildings with students. We started out with 95 percent occupancy and I questioned why that could not be 100 percent. Well, I learned things as I went along, and one was that you always lose some students between the fall and spring semesters. We needed to grow the freshmen class and have more sophomores living in the new dormitories. We stopped one short of the number of dormitories we had originally planned to construct. When Blanding and Kirwan Towers come down, UK can decide at that time if another dormitory is feasible.

I hope that all of these new residence halls, built almost simultaneously, do not become a burden for the university thirty or forty years from now. We did put in a reserve against maintenance, which we did not have on the older dormitories. Previously, when it came time to do maintenance, the funds to pay for it had to be found somewhere. In this case, there is a reserve set aside annually out of the revenue for maintenance.

I believe the entire residence hall process worked really well. Randy Churchey, the CEO of EdR, and I talk periodically. I was involved much more in the first contracts than the last ones because Eric Monday, executive vice president for finance and administration, came on board and does an excellent job. It became easier for Monday to deal with EdR than me. I had gotten pretty close to Randy Churchey and he would come to Lexington for football games and Keeneland. It was much better that I stepped away from negotiations. But I really value that project and it proved to be a great way to keep me busy during the years I worked on it.

Overall, I commend UK for the progress made during the past several years. UK is able to attract good students and excellent faculty. We have a state that, no matter how much we may want it to do more, is still somewhat supportive of higher education, considering all of Kentucky's economic challenges. I believe that we seem to have the right leaders at the right time in key positions at UK, and I am generally very hopeful about the future of UK, which has to be a lot of things to a lot of different people. But I suspect that UK has a 95 percent approval level among Kentuckians. A person out in the state might not like how the quarterback is playing or how some issues within the university are being handled, but if you asked a hundred random Kentuckians about UK, I believe ninety-five of them would say more good things than bad about the university. Now, of course that would not apply to UK employees, who generally have their own grievances from salaries to parking.

For me, the opportunity to serve on the UK Board was an offer I could not refuse. One has to come into something like service on the board prepared to participate and make some positive contributions. Also, I think I would tell any prospective UK board members that it is not a place to advance their own agendas. I know people who have gone on the board of a company because they thought maybe it would be good for their business—and that is not necessarily frowned upon in the corporate world. If an opportunity were to arise, there they would be, standing at the front of the line. I am sure there have been people who have gone on boards to become suppliers and so forth. But it does not work that way with the UK Board because it is already too fragmented. If one begins to promote one's own agenda on the board, the perception is negative even if one's actions are not.

The biggest negative regarding the UK Board I saw were people who joined the board but did not have time to commit to it. They did not come to educational programs or any campus events beyond board meetings. They might have had pretty good attendance at the board meetings, but they would arrive fifteen minutes before the meeting and leave before it was over. Board members like that were most discouraging because no matter how capable they were, they were not getting much out of it and UK got very little out of them. Sadly, there always seems to be people like that on the board. It is more of a commitment than one might think it would be.

Chapter Seven

Reflections

*Looking back over the years,
I think I probably needed a little more balance
in my life. Perhaps I drove a little bit harder
on the career side than I had to.*

At this point in my life I now have the time to enjoy my four grandchildren. I have become close to them and I hope they will all have a pretty good opinion of me. However, I would say that anybody who knows me and reads this memoir, including my grandchildren, will be surprised because writing it has also surprised me. I realized as I wrote that I have never discussed many of these subjects with my family. Over the years the events of our lives unfolded and we simply enjoyed being together. Perhaps because of the extensive travel my work required, the professional side of my life seemed more apart from my home life than might normally be the case. However, I believe that, as my grandchildren complete their educations and begin their own independent lives and careers, they will be in a much better position to reflect on what I have shared within these pages.

Looking back over the years, I think I probably needed a little more balance in my life. Perhaps I drove a little bit harder on the career side than I had to. I was the guy who got his mail while on vacation. I not only took phone calls on days off but I also initiated work calls. I believe we should all try to accomplish something during the life we are given, whatever those accomplishments may be. But I also know one can lead a more balanced life than I have. I was fortunate to have people around me who either understood my life choices or just put up with them. If I had it to do over again, I would strive for a more equal work/life balance.

I have always been the type of person who, if committed to something, took it on fully. When I went to Textron I knew I would be there for about a ten-year run. I talked with Gay about the move and told her that while at Textron I would not be able to raise my head very often from my work. At least I warned her ahead of time. But I am the same way about everything. If I decide that I should not eat red meat, then I do not eat *any* red meat. Somebody might say, "Well, you can have so many ounces of red meat every once in a while." Well, by my way of thinking, if am going to eat red meat, I will eat as much as I want; if I am not going to, I won't have any. That trait of mine also affected how I approached the business side of my life.

I never really had to worry about finances. I was not wealthy until late in my career but I had no debt coming out of college. If one is debt free, one can have a little more patience in making career choices. I also married later in life than was the norm in those days. I was twenty-five when Gay and I married, and it helped that I had been working for two or three years prior to our marriage.

If I were to offer a young person career advice, I would encourage them to look closely at prospective fields to pursue. One should learn if a prospective field is moving in a positive direction and has historically been strong. For a young person, that type of review might be hard to accomplish. But if one goes to a company or firm that has skated along looking at bankruptcy, or has a history of big layoffs and work disruptions, there is a risk of being caught up in a failing enterprise regardless of how good one is or how hard one works.

I consider myself lucky because I went with a family company that I knew very little about other than that the owners lived in a much better section of Maysville than the Hardymons. But then Browning Manufacturing was acquired by Emerson Electric, a much, much larger company that had what was called at that time an AAA financial credit rating. I had a good education and had experienced some good mentoring, but it was my connection with Emerson that had the biggest impact on my life and career.

During most of my time at Emerson Electric I never considered changing companies. The thought just never crossed my mind. I assumed I would spend my entire career with Emerson. Perhaps that view is more typical of people in the Midwest and South. In today's business climate it is best to keep one's options open to periodic career changes.

An important skill young people need to develop is the ability to make good public presentations. If you can stand up and explain what you are doing and what you would like to do, that will move you further than some other skills might. My college education did not adequately prepare me for public speaking. I suppose an engineer was considered an eyeshade and a grinder who would not need to speak in public very often. I had to learn how to present, and fortunately I had people suggest to me that I get professional help, which I did rather early in my career.

During my career I found that preparation was one of the most important factors in success. I never went to bed without being conscious of what was going to be required the next day. I was surprised occasionally, but I spent a lot of time preparing, whether it was doing my lessons in high school and college or getting ready to make a presentation on Wall Street. I was big on run-throughs so that I had a basic idea of what might happen. Then, if a surprise occurred, I at least had that preparation to fall back on.

It may seem obvious, but maintaining one's health is vital. Regardless of how good you are at your job you have to be there. There have been some awfully gifted people who unfortunately did not maintain good health to support their capabilities and accomplishments. With good health comes energy, stamina, and the ability to participate. I have always said, "If you are prepared, then you are present. When you are present, you can participate." I am very fortunate that I still have good health, which allows me to schedule nearly every minute of my day. I am not doing anything as difficult as I used to do, but I still try to keep going and that is a plus.

I am not as patient as perhaps I should be, but then I am also not as impatient as some people I have known. For example, I can be impatient when a traffic signal takes too long to turn green. My great mentor Chuck Knight said that sometimes I made a decision before we had thought everything through. But in turn, when I had some big things to decide, like moving from Emerson to Textron, I went through a five-month process trying to decide if that was what I should do. For certain things I have more patience than people realize. But throughput is important to me. I will watch people to see how they do in getting the job done, making their point, and moving on. I know I may have occasionally offended a trustee at the University of Kentucky by cutting them off and suggesting that they get to the point. I believed that was a better way to run a meeting and hopefully I did not upset too many board members.

Over the course of my career I did not have many decisions to make about what came next. I made the decision to leave the Kentucky Highway Department and go to Browning Manufacturing without looking into or interviewing with any other company. I was simply asked by a former neighbor in Maysville, who ended up being my boss, if I wanted to interview for a position at Browning. I drove from Lexington to Maysville one Saturday morning, sat for an interview, and within a few days was offered a position that I accepted.

Likewise, there was very little difficulty involved when I opted to go to St. Louis to be a division president at Emerson Electric. Sometimes you have to decide if you are going to stay in a position for the rest of your life or make a change. That can be dangerous because the decision to stay can put a label on you. The other option is to move, so I decided to move. When I went to Chicago, I stayed with the same company but I still had to decide whether to stay in St. Louis and keep doing what I was doing or move. When I went back to St. Louis it was an easy decision because there was not going to be a job in Chicago. I was told that Emerson was promoting me to a position in St. Louis and they already knew who would take my place in Chicago.

But it was a huge and difficult decision to leave Emerson for Textron. I did that for two reasons. First, I knew that my best contribution in management would be with a multi-industry company. Second, I knew I was not going to be a true CEO if I stayed with Emerson. Neither money nor location was a factor in my decision. I enjoyed living in St. Louis, but by then our children were grown and out on their own so we were free to move without disrupting the family.

I wanted to be a CEO because the people I looked up to the most were the leaders of their companies. I wanted to at least try to get to a somewhat comparable level in an organization. Whether that meant I was at an equal level in doing the job or not, that was something else. But I was committed to becoming a CEO. I had a number of people encourage me to look at other companies before I ever accepted an interview with Textron. I only had one other realistic chance that I knew of with a company that was looking for a CEO. If I had pursued that option, I think I would at least have been brought in for one of the final interviews. The rest of the opportunities, where I did not move further in the interview process, were just recruiters putting a book together with probably twenty-five or more prospects for the available position.

I had a very secure position at Emerson because I had proven myself. I had been with the company so many years that they were not likely to ask me to do anything differently, whether more or less. Emerson was known for people staying with them for a long time, and that is another thing you should look for when you are evaluating a company. Textron did not have a reputation for employee longevity, so it was a little riskier career move.

Many people, more today than then, think that CEO positions should not be held by people sixty-five or older because they are not in a position to be making five-year plans. I was almost fifty-five when I joined Textron and I did not officially get the CEO position for another fifteen months. So believing I would be at Textron nine-plus years might have been assuming a little too much, even though it ultimately worked out that way.

If I had become CEO at age fifty, I would not have done as good a job. I needed those years of experience between 1983, when I came back from Chicago to the corporate office, and 1989, when I went to Textron. Those years taught me what the job as CEO is all about. I could not grasp the full picture from my previous vantage points within the company. The timing of becoming CEO worked out exceedingly well for me. The job did not wear me down. My enthusiasm about being named the Textron CEO was as high the day I left as it was the day I began.

Deciding when to leave a company is a difficult decision. I went through a period at Textron where there was some uncertainty among a few of the board members and staff about whether or not I should leave at a particular time. They wanted me to stay on and one can get a little intoxicated by that type of flattery. But once I started down the road to leave, a month or two later I was all set on going forward with my decision.

I was very fortunate in that, almost immediately upon leaving Textron, I had many opportunities to serve on boards. My calendar stayed fairly full and in many aspects it seemed like I was doing the same things I had done at Textron. The big difference was I would go to a company at a different location, like Allentown, Pennsylvania, or Richmond, Virginia, rather than stay in one place. It did not take me very long to feel good about moving into the next chapter of my career.

Everyone should realize that life can change in an instant. That instant for me was when my doctor told me I had prostate cancer. Thankfully, the diagnosis came after I had retired because I know I did a better job of recovering than I would have been able to as CEO. Also, I would have been less productive for the company than I would have wanted to be. That conflict would have been difficult for me to handle.

Regarding my cancer, I was very fortunate to have had good

people around me because I was in denial. I had been getting regular physicals, with everything checking out fine. But after one physical, I received a call from the Lahey Clinic in Boston telling me I had an elevated prostate-specific antigen (PSA). They had a policy that if the PSA is substantially elevated from one test to another they would do a biopsy. I went up to Lahey Clinic, had the biopsy done, and left. I never anticipated that there would be any problem with that biopsy. But when they called, they told me that of the six places where they had performed the biopsy, one of them was cancerous. They gave me a rating that tells you how severe the cancer is at that point, and mine was right in the middle. I returned to Lahey and they took me through everything that could be done. Doing nothing is one alternative when you are almost sixty-five. I talked to Charles Wethington, more as a friend than anything else, and he got me in touch with Dr. Randy Rowland at UK Healthcare.

It seemed obvious that at my age, and with overall good health, I should take some action, and that is what I did. They performed some additional blood tests and then one day I found myself sitting in a hospital room at UK waiting for surgery. I remember thinking to myself, "What am I doing here? I got up this morning, and I worked out on the treadmill. I don't feel sick!"

Once the surgery was over I had another two- or three-day wait. Everything about the process seemed to take two or three days. Dr. Rowland then told me that the surrounding areas did not show any other problems, and soon I was up and about again. I remember there was a week where I could not drive, but I participated in a Lexmark board meeting by phone even though I was in Lexington.

I now encourage everyone to take prostate cancer seriously and seek treatment immediately. I once had a friend come into my office in tears to tell me he had prostate cancer. He could not be consoled at the time but since then he has received treatment and has done well. The last time I played golf with him he was more concerned about his bad knees.

As a native Kentuckian and someone who cares about the future of our Commonwealth, I must say I do not have a lot of hope for Kentucky improving its relative position in the nation's economy, education, or healthcare. There is no silver bullet to fix all of Kentucky's problems. But I believe it would be helpful if Kentucky had a business plan. Of course, some criticized UK president Lee T. Todd's "Top-Twenty Business Plan" to make the university a top-twenty university by 2020. Many were skeptical, and for good reason, that the state or anyone else would ever provide the funds necessary to reach that goal. My response to President Todd's plan was to simply remove the time restraint of 2020 and keep reporting against what we were trying to achieve. That process alone will cause an institution to improve. UK will not achieve top-twenty status nationally by 2020, but it helped to have that as a goal.

So what can Kentucky do to begin targeting areas that desperately need improvement? Some places have focused on digital initiatives. Others have focused on automotive supply, which probably has not proven to be the best move even though many thought it was at the time. But in Kentucky we go from touting batteries one day to automotive the next day and to steel or aluminum the next.

Quite frankly, just from the time I have spent around the governor's office, I do not see how a governor has time to think about economic development. Perhaps the governor's staff has time to help in that area; I simply do not know. Moreover, the governor has a four-year term and two years into being governor they have to begin a reelection campaign. There is a built-in limit to how long anyone will listen to their strategic plan. But it would seem to me that instead of trying to say the state is forty-third in this and fortieth in that, Kentucky should aim for something higher.

Being from the northeastern region of the state, I think governors have spent far too much time trying to completely change eastern Kentucky. The state already has a vibrant and productive region in the triangle between Cincinnati, Louisville, and Lexington and to an extent around Bowling Green in southern Kentucky. Perhaps it would make more sense to put more resources into the regions that are already growing to increase revenue that could be targeted to help more depressed regions within Kentucky.

In regard to the University of Kentucky, I do think our research dollars should be focused a little more around the state. It is obvious UK should be a leader in equine research. In medical research, UK is heavily involved with cancer, Alzheimer's, and aging. Of course, as UK is a land-grant university, agriculture has always been a large part of its mission, and agricultural research is beginning to think outside of its own walls more than when I first became involved on UK's Board of Trustees. I believe that UK should look to help these areas of strength even more.

President Lee Todd underestimated how difficult it would be to change Kentucky. When he first became president, he often spoke passionately about the "Kentucky uglies," sociocultural aspects of Kentuckians that hold individuals and the state back. Most people understand what the "uglies" are, but it is nevertheless a long struggle to improve them. Moreover, if a person chooses behavior like smoking, that habit actually contributes to the Kentucky uglies and makes change even harder. It is extremely difficult to move the meter when it comes to most of Kentucky's biggest and most intransigent problems.

Some people are going to always resist help even if someone or some agency is trying to help them with their health, their weight, their education, or their children's health and education. They resist because they do not want to be told what to do. Physical trainers have told me there are two or three reasons why people do not exercise more: it takes too much time, they cannot afford it, or they simply do not like it. But one of the biggest reasons is that people do not like being told what to do and physical trainers tell you what to do. Following orders like that is not a Kentucky thing.

But Kentucky got into this difficult position by being primarily an agricultural state and not moving beyond agriculture to the extent that, for example, North Carolina has. We must ask ourselves how and why that happened. Comparing Kentucky and North Carolina, we should draw a line and ask, "Where did we separate?" If you look at the histories of both states, there is no reason why North Carolina should be any more advanced or prosperous than Kentucky.

The only real disappointment I had in my entire experience with Textron was that the stock price declined after I left. The method of running the company as an operating company versus a holding company did not stick, and it reverted back to where it had been. The roots were just too deep for my staff and me to change permanently. But the process worked for Emerson Electric and it has worked for other companies. It probably would have worked for Textron. If I were younger I would like the opportunity to go back and try again, even though I am not sure if a second try would make any difference. I would need to have someone designated to follow me as CEO who really believed in the process, and not just say they believed in it. It is only natural that new leadership changes things.

Since my days at Emerson, I have had sufficient wealth. My first concern has always been to take care of my family. Beyond that I have become very involved in philanthropy. The burning motivation behind my philanthropy is a concern, or perhaps a question, as to why I have had this success while others have not. It is like the often asked question regarding people in accidents. Why did one person die and another survive? I remember going to India and seeing those young children running around between the cars on the road begging for handouts. They barely had on enough clothes to cover themselves. It reminded me that when and where one is born makes a huge difference, regardless of any other factors. That experience, and others like it, motivated me to want to help others even more.

That said, I do not want to sugarcoat my philanthropy too much. After retiring from Textron and coming into a large payout in stocks from my incentive plan, I knew how much money I had based on the value of the stocks. At that point I began working with investors and we went through the value of my estate step by step. Eventually, the investors asked, "What are you going to do with this money?" Of course, there were alternatives based on tax advantages if nothing else. I established the Hardymon Family Foundation at least in part because of the tax motivation to do so. Money is set aside for the foundation and there is a limit to how much money I can give each year to build it up. I can put any amount I want into the fund but I only get tax relief based on a certain amount. There is no limit to the amount of funds going out. I created a family foundation because I wanted my children to understand that the foundation has a specified mission regarding what it will support. For example, when I see a person standing on a street corner begging for money, I am moved to want to do something right then and there regardless of how that person came to be destitute. Nevertheless, I knew I had to narrow the scope of our philanthropy, and so we chose education.

At the time my family consisted of me, Gay, and our two adult children. I felt we had to establish some kind of controls regarding where our money went, or at least some overarching guidelines. If that is not done, inevitably you see an article in the newspaper saying someone needs help with their rent or something similar. Anyone with empathy would feel moved to help with those types of situations and without guidelines might be sending checks hither and yon. So I limited our foundation to mostly providing support for educational needs, which has worked out well. Over the years we have been involved in giving to a number of schools because we now have more family members with degrees from a variety of schools, including Kentucky, Missouri, Georgia Tech, Georgia, and Penn State.

I think the main incentive is to give where you have an interest and where you think you can make a difference. Of course, I realize I am asked to be involved in some not-for-profit organizations and institutions because they expect a donation. Over time, I have come to resent this practice. I went through a period where I went on some boards, like the Kentucky History Center, for example, when I had no more background for that board than the man in the moon.

Over the years I have been very fortunate to be able to give back to the University of Kentucky through a variety of projects. It is very personally gratifying to see firsthand how those gifts have helped the university. One of my first major gifts came when President Wethington asked me to support the construction of brick and stone signage at several entrances to the university campus. While that marked the beginning of my philanthropy, subsequently one gift led to another. I supported the construction of the first building in UK's Digital Village on the north side of campus. Having my name placed on that prominent building at UK has haunted me somewhat. I am not sure how much one should give to have that type of recognition. I always assumed that anyone who had a building named for them had led a very successful life and was dead.

I am a firm believer that one of UK's most pressing and continuing needs is better facilities. I supported the second building in UK's Digital Village, which is now the Davis Marksbury Building. I also contributed to the rebuilding of the Main Building after a devastating fire nearly destroyed it in 2001. After supporting other building projects, I became increasingly interested in supporting the new hospital.

For the most part, the rest of my gifts to UK have been one-shot smaller gifts compared to the facilities gifts. It has become a little embarrassing that my name is on so many things at UK, but they are all projects I believed in and was pleased to support. Most recently, a floor in the Markey Cancer Center has been named for Gay and me as well as the new James and Gay Hardymon Center for Student Success in the College of Engineering. I would have been sufficiently recognized if they had stopped with the naming of the Hardymon Building in the Digital Village. I really did not need my name to be anywhere else. But I am told that seeing names like mine on places and plaques encourages others to give to UK. If that is true we can handle the embarrassment of too many acknowledgments.

I have been asked what it feels like to be able to make gifts to places I want to help. Well, in a way, I feel it is necessary to give after coming into such a significant amount of money. In my case it has really been about timing. When the Textron Board came up with the idea in 1992 to give me stock options equal to what I would get by the time I became sixty-five, they had no idea that stock was going to go up as much as it did. Part of the reason the stock price went up might be that we ran the company well. But another major reason was the world economy was in better shape than it had ever been for those ten years in the 1990s. That was important to keep in mind because otherwise, I might have begun to think more highly of myself than was justified! But my good financial situation resulted in large part simply from timing.

So upon receiving a financial windfall, I naturally began thinking about my family and what I might do for my children and grandchildren. Of course, I knew that one has more incentive to climb that ladder when you do not have money. So I do not talk to them about it. I discuss financial issues primarily with my daughter and son and they can then convey to their spouses and children what they choose. A lot of what I am giving my children now is what is allowed by the tax laws. There is a limit to how much they can take out of these trusts. Bessemer, which manages the trusts, has the right to turn them down if they choose. So if either of my children were to start having trouble with alcohol, drugs, or something that alters or harms their judgment, Besse-mer can decide to turn them down. That keeps me out of the deci-sion-making process. Once I give the money to the trust, I have no say in how it is spent. Bessemer works closely with my daughter and son to help them become better investors and to understand there are certain instances when you might not want to pull mon-ey out of the trust. They encourage them to borrow money while interest rates remain at record lows. They can even borrow mon-ey from their Bessemer Trust.

But regarding how it feels to be a philanthropist, ironically, about a year ago, for the first time, I made a gift primarily because I could. I have given to churches in the past and there are three churches that I still give to each year. Lexington's Central Christian Church began a development effort to renovate its education building, which provides space for the Sunday school classes and church offices. They wanted to put together a capital campaign for the project and a person I had never met before, one of the associate ministers, came to see me. I listened to his pitch, took out my checkbook, and wrote him a check for $50,000. And I was sober when I did it! I think that was the first gift I made just because I could.

Occasionally someone who knew about my philanthropy would ask me about it. For example, Don Jacobs spent a lot of time talking to me about the gifts I had made over the years. Don also had the capacity to make large gifts, but he was curious about my motivation to give. I remember we were in a golf cart when he first asked me how I decided where to give. After I explained to Don my process for making those decisions, he said to me, "I'm going to make a meaningful gift" and he did. Don was not a UK graduate but he made a major gift for the new science building, which is now named for Don and his wife Cathy. He also made other significant gifts in recent years to the Hope Center in Lexington and to other places. A lot can happen in a golf cart. I could do a show called *Philanthropists in Golf Carts* modeled after *Comedians in Cars* with Jerry Seinfeld.

William T. Young was a tremendous philanthropist with his own money. But he also worked hard to convince others to give to causes he supported. He did that in a nice way and got it done. I do not have any interest in raising money from other people. I still serve on some UK fundraising committees and I am told that my presence encourages others to give. If that is true, then I am happy to help. I am honored to be in a position to benefit others.

While preparing this memoir I lost my wife and partner of fifty-eight years. Gay Garred Hardymon stood with me though graduate school, military service, cross-country moves, long absences from home, and all of the ups and downs of a life journey. Gay raised our two children, ran the household, and served as my confidante and advisor. She made anywhere we lived feel like our home. Whatever my accomplishments, I could not have achieved them without Gay's strong and unwavering support.

My two grown children, Jennifer Hardymon Sovich and Frank Hardymon, have each pursued their dreams and ambitions and have raised families of their own. I am blessed with four wonderful grandchildren: Caroline Sovich Branham and Christopher Sovich and Emma and Grace Hardymon. All are doing well, with promising futures.

It is somewhat intimidating, and yet joyous, to look back on one's life and recall all those family members, friends, and colleagues who have helped raise me, educate me, mentor me, encourage me, push me, and share life's experiences with me. Life is about preparing oneself to be ready when opportunity knocks. Growing up in small-town Kentucky or even as a student at the university, I could never have imagined the course my life would take. It has been a wondrous and very satisfying ride. And, as I have done my entire life, I cannot wait to see what happens tomorrow because I plan to be ready.